LIVING THE ETHNOGRAPHIC LIFE

DAN ROSE
University of Pennsylvania

Qualitative Research Methods
Volume 23

SAGE PUBLICATIONS
The International Professional Publishers
Newbury Park   London   New Delhi

Copyright © 1990 by Sage Publications, Inc.

For information address:

SAGE Publications, Inc.
2455 Teller Road
Newbury Park, California 91320

SAGE Publications Ltd.
6 Bonhill Street
London EC2A 4PU
United Kingdom

SAGE Publications India Pvt. Ltd.
M-32 Market
Greater Kailash I
New Delhi 110 048 India

Printed in the United States of America

Library of Congress Cataloging-in-Publication Data

Rose, Dan
    Living the ethnographic life / Dan Rose.
      p.   cm. -- (Qualitative research methods : 23)
    Includes bibliographical references.
    ISBN 0-8039-3998-1 (C). -- ISBN 0-8039-3999-X (P)
    1. Ethnology--Methodology. 2. Ethnology--Fieldwork. I. Title.
II. Series: Qualitative research methods : v. 23.
GN345.R668 1990
305.8'0072--dc20   90-8775
                                                             CIP

FIRST PRINTING, 1990
Sage Production Editor: Judith L. Hunter

CONTENTS

EDITORS' INTRODUCTION

The postmodern moment has arrived in the social sciences. Its presence is especially felt in qualitative research circles where calls for new forms of ethnography, polyvocal texts, multigenre narratives, impressionistic tales, cinematic reconstructions, lyrical sociology, and poetic anthropology are prominent. There are, of course, at least as many reasonable justifications for textual experimentation as there are advocates for alterations; but all calls for reform — modest or sweeping — point to a growing lack of confidence among readers across the social sciences with traditional research and reporting styles. Critics argue that conventional social research dulls the imagination; locks the observed inside rigid category systems having little or nothing to do with the culture of the researched, but everything to do with our research culture; promotes an insidious institutionalization of social boundaries that separate "us" (the observers) from "them" (the observed); and perhaps most telling has become rather tedious, if not boring, thus losing its power to convince.

To some alert to the postmodern scene, change will come about only by the thoughtful and sharp reconstruction of reporting practices. They believe that lack of style, not substance, is what currently ails social research. To others, the matter goes far deeper. Meaningful change in style can only come about by altering in a fundamental way our taken-for-granted research practices. The enterprise itself has become socially and intellectually suspect, and the only proper postmodern response is to break from received traditions and institutionally situated realities. The text of the future not only will look different but also it will be constructed on different grounds than those of the past.

Dan Rose stands clearly in the radical camp on these matters. *Living the Ethnographic Life* is an argument for a bold shift in ethnographic perspective. It is a passionate argument as well. For Dan Rose, it is not enough to tinker with our writing styles, take voice lessons, develop plot plans, study art, or play with our tables of contents. We must redefine the ethnographic project itself. Such a redefinition requires both a sense of history and a sense of the possibilities future work allows.

In terms of history, Dan Rose argues that ethnography is linked closely to corporate purposes, academic and economic. He suggests our traditions are such that pretextual assumptions passed from one generation to the next more or less determine what it is we experience in the worlds we investigate and, therefore, what it is we can say about these worlds. In terms of the future, our link to the past must be broken experientially by reversing our methodological practices. Such reversals would foster ethnographies of intimacy, not distance; of stories, not models; of possibilities, not stabilities; and of contingent understandings, not detachable conclusions.

Cutting the ties that bind and preserve is painful to be sure, but as Dan Rose shows through examples of contemporary work—his own and others—there is precedent for such genre-busting ethnography. There is also considerable rhyme and reason behind such work. This is a breathless monograph. It is as ambitious as it is swift. But from the work comes a broad outline of just what living the ethnographic life might entail (and detail).

—John Van Maanen
Peter K. Manning
Marc L. Miller

ACKNOWLEDGMENTS

Permission to reprint from the following is gratefully acknowledged:

"Amid Animal Skins and Family Pride, A Youth Becomes Swazi King," by Michael Parks, copyright 1990, Los Angeles Times. Reprinted by permission.

"Through a Soviet Lens: Gomorrah on Hudson," by Philip Taubman and "Zaire Now Dancing to Different Beat," by Edward A. Gargan, copyright © 1986 by The New York Times Company. Reprinted by permission.

Liner notes from "Einstein on the Beach," Sony Classical U.S.A.

On the Rim of the Curve, by Michael Cook, copyright by the author and Breakwater Books, Limited, St. Johns, Newfoundland. Reprinted by permission.

Eskimo, by Stanley Diamond, copyright by the author, permission from Open Book, an imprint of Station Hill Press, Barrytown, NY, 12507

Thanks to Ivan Brady for permission to reprint "Reversal" from *Anthropological Poetics*, edited by him and published by Rowman and Littlefield, Savage, MD, 1990, and to Paul Benson for permission to reprint "Ethnography as a Form of Life," which appeared in the *Journal of the Steward Anthropological Society* 17, 1 & 2, 1987-1988 (copyright 1990).

"I am the Reasonable One," by Rosario Morales, is reproduced by permission of the American Anthropological Association from *Reflections* (1985).

Excerpts from "Easing In" and "When My Picture Disappears," by Aqqaluk Lynge, are reproduced by permission of the American Anthropological Association from *Reflections*.

LIVING THE ETHNOGRAPHIC LIFE

DAN ROSE
University of Pennsylvania

1. FORM OF LIFE

One can readily imagine that the corpus of anthropological work, with some minor exceptions, will in some future, more clear-sighted time, be perceived as little more than a reflection of the attitudes and the intellectual play of an imperial civilization. And the record will reveal, I think, that anthropologists had only the most abstract interest in the cultures they studied. (Diamond, 1980, p. 8)

It should be clear then that much of the talk about reform and change from the point of view of white South Africa in general is premised not on what the whites of South Africa may have to unlearn, but on what black people, those 'prospective citizens of the Republic,' need to be speedily introduced to so that they can become 'responsible' citizens of the future, so that they can become westerners in black skins. In a nutshell, the entire ideology of reform is based on the 'humanization' of the oppressed according to the specifications of South African capital, which, itself, is governed according to the specifications of the international corporate world.

The practical aspects of this modern form of colonial 'pacification' imply the implementation of modern principles of business management. (Ndebele, 1987, pp. 225-226)

10

> For certainly the development of social anthropology in England is linked to the spread of our colonial empire and its administrative, missionary and commercial needs. (Evans-Pritchard, 1969, p. x).

This book is a critique and a reminder. It critiques the bureaucratic lives we as ethnographers lead and shows how our corporate way of living constrains our pursuit of ethnographic knowledge. To emphasize the critical approach on the way our lives of qualitative inquiry have evolved over the past 400 years of market culture, I have read from the history of the formation of Anglo-American corporations (Section 9 in this chapter). Through some of Shakespeare's plays we can visualize the stage set of early English capital-ism — that complex bundle of practices and legally binding discourses — in its extensive global geography. Because ethnography grew up with the colonizing praxis of capitalist culture, I draw briefly from the history of its literature, explorers' travels, and corporate history to mark the passage and to help reveal the social forms such as the incorporated university that literally, textually, and legally frame the way we do the business of ethnog-raphy today.

The reminder in the second chapter on reversal takes us back to one of the promising, radical projects of nineteenth century ethnography. At its best it meant to take us over to the other side, to take up, return, and then textualize the other points of view insofar as possible, even to risk assimilation with those studied. It is the potential in reversal that is proposed as an antidote to the corporate-bureaucratized ethnographic inquiry we pursue. The last sec-tion is both about taking chances with our lives and inhabiting a more democratic epistemology. By democratic epistemology is meant in part that the thinking of the ethnographer and those studied inhabit the same histori-cal moment.

Within anthropology there has been interest in reversing the academic perspective by using native epistemologies to critique our own assumptions (Lutz, 1988; Marcus & Cushman, 1982) and thereby help establish a larger humanity that includes our historical differences as differences within a more comprehensive intercultural discourse. Sociologists have expressed concern for a penetrating critique of existing categories and received ap-proaches to the emotions, drug use, delinquency, AIDS, gender research, and other social challenges that are far from being understood adequately in today's society. Although this monograph is written primarily for anthropol-ogists, sociological participant observers and other disciplinary ethnographers share common challenges and their collective contributions influence the various practitioners.

Living the Ethnographic Life through the reading of academic and poetic sources joins other works of social scientists in urging a more radical democratization of knowledge, one that simultaneously deprivileges our academic inquiry while serving to help recover ideas and practices from other points of view—whether of marginal or oppressed people, whether close to home or geographically and culturally remote (see Jackson, 1989; Stoller, 1989b).

Sections 1 and 2 were drafted together as a further investigation during the writing of my book *Black American Street Life* (Rose, 1987). The ethnographic research on which that book was written addressed disciplinary, ethical, moral, personal, and career problems that have challenged many of us as some of the most sensitive issues in the human sciences (Bulmer, 1982; Said, 1989).

Research for that book was covert. At the urging of Erving Goffman I lived and worked with welfare- and working-class African-Americans without disclosing my identity as an ethnographer who was documenting their lives. His reasons for directing me toward such an ethically painful choice were compelling. He suggested taking a job in the community and living and identifying solely with blacks; he argued that I might learn far more about everyday life than typically had been discovered by hanging out or using questionnaires. With painful resistance I finally agreed with him, became an auto mechanic for a man, rented an apartment next door to his auto repair shop, and lived virtually on the street for two years, hustling and being hustled, working and playing in the daily round without disclosing my identity as an ethnographer. Much of the time I tried to mimic the lives of the black men with whom I worked and drank.

Covert inquiry and the intimacy of engagement it facilitated fatally subverted my received assumptions about the practices of ethnographers. For example, I could not use a questionnaire; photograph or tape record anyone; take down notes in public on interesting happenings; ask leading or pointed (rude) questions of who, why, how, when, or where; and I could not rely on my sacred status of knowledgeable anthropologist to get me out of trouble when I was challenged to fight, or when I tried to outhustle someone and was expected to pay the consequences. Indeed, given the ethical dimensions of my choice, the difficult emotions that attended deception, and the maddening frustration of not carrying out the scientific method in which I had been trained by books, seminars, professors, and graduate student colleagues, my entire field stay was haunted sharply by a sense of intellectual and moral failure: I couldn't gather "data" (for a fuller account, see Rose, 1987).

On reflection, while writing *Black American Street Life* a compulsion grew to explore further than that book allowed the culture of American corporations that frame our academic everyday lives, the texts by which we live and conduct research, and to open myself to the possibilities for a poetic of inquiry that simultaneously shatters and responds to a distressed methodology that secret investigations can give rise to.

Here, then, is a move toward a methodological treatise. It urges a moral and aesthetic practice: Do radical ethnography, one that gets you closer to those you study at the risk of going native and never returning; it is hoped, at least, that you will not again embrace the received assumptions with which you, inheriting your academic texts, methods, and corporate academic culture, began.

The absurdity of that last sentence in the admonition, however, is lost on none of us. If we study prisoners or criminals, *Fortune* 500 CEOs or members of world parliaments, middle-class working women who suffer repeated spontaneous abortions, or industrial polluters, we have to ask how far we as ethnographers ought to go toward living their lives alongside them and then crafting in textual discourse what we have learned.

That is one of the pressing questions.

There is a sense in which we are all ethnographers now: persons, genders, groups, agencies, villages, suburbs, occupational groups, classes, corporations, countries, trying to write about our collective selves for others or gathering what others say and interpreting what it means that there are those different than we are (Dorst, 1989). *Living the Ethnographic Life* questions this space of difference in which the inquiring self has proved to be as problematic as social and cultural others.

* * *

As I began living with the African-Americans in Philadelphia, the American cities of the late 1960s still were addressing the emotional issues raised by the confrontations between black people and the police, and the burning of neighborhoods in one of the most dramatic forms of social protest in American history. Anthropology departments at that time were polarized politically. In some departments the hostility between students and faculty centered on such issues as Vietnam, but most immediately faculty were criticized for the lack of relevance anthropology had shown to the peoples it had studied in a postcolonial era of western economic hegemony. Criticism was also leveled at anthropology for its failure to engage socially, politically, and intellectually the issues facing the country—civil rights and citizenship, our own complex streams of cultures, and the problems of identity and domination in the so-called melting pot.

I chose my doctoral dissertation fieldwork site partly in response to the student critique of those times, in an effort to make my anthropological training of critical relevance to the country. In South Philadelphia—where I took up residence, lived on the street in the summer, did pick-up work, and finally free-lanced as an underemployed handyman like others who lived in the area—I transcribed field notes at night sometimes too drunk to focus well, or worked on them the next morning, more sober and less close to what had gone on the day before.

Because I did not disclose my identity and reside officially as an anthropologist present only to study the people, what occurred was a collapse of the role distance between my neighbors and myself. I had no identity, no status to hide behind except what I could pick up locally. As with several of my men friends there I became an urban adventurer, wandering through the city at nights creating minor adventures that ended sometimes early in the mornings, drunk and worn out. At first I worked 12-hour days in the repair shop and there was exhausted by the sheer madness of trying to repair autos with poor tools, low-level skills, and the frustrated motivations of an ethnographic field-worker.

The fact that I did not say explicitly that I was conducting anthropological fieldwork led rapidly to a disintegration of my assumptions about what information I could gather. I feared that what was occurring was a complete lack of matchup between what I had read in graduate school and the entries in my fieldnotes. At the time I could think of no greater anxiety.

Over the years I felt that the logic of inquiry that I had learned from a graduate education of reading, seminars, and talking had been detonated by the field experience. Ethnography as knowledge about our own culture or about others opened up for me as a *radically fractured* way of life. My assumptions derived from reading ethnographies could not be played out in the field given the covertness, lack of explicitness, and lack of the sacred status claimed by ethnographers for their inquisitive role.

The received logic of inquiry, which could be expanded further, can be evoked by a diagram with arrows (see Figure 1.1). The words represent an

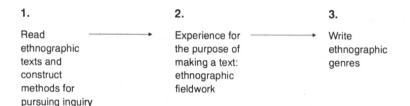

1.

Read ethnographic texts and construct methods for pursuing inquiry

2.

Experience for the purpose of making a text: ethnographic fieldwork

3.

Write ethnographic genres

Figure 1.1

ethnographer's activity, and the arrow (a line) indicates not so much causality as logical progression.

First, one becomes socialized in graduate school to one's profession, to the conduct of ethnography. The whole aim of this socialization is at one level to duplicate the achievements of the discipline, and at another level to contribute uniquely to the growth and development of knowledge. Second, one conducts inquiry along the lines one has read. I simplify, of course, but it is as if doing ethnography is to construct a text from the experiences with others, experiences carefully controlled by the profession. In a strong sense all experiences were laid out normatively in advance by peers, professors, monographs, articles, and books. In addition, one carefully grooms a persona, an identity that conforms to the expectations, but becomes the persona necessary to engage in certain experiences and to craft the expected texts. Our texts are forms of how we know. If inquiry does not conform to the disciplinary texts one has read, the terrible reality — at least the fear — is that one's experiences will not be relevant for the texts one will write.

Third, the success in crafting a text has everything to do with a career because, with a few exceptions, careers are text-dependent. We write to be recognized and promoted, but we write also to confirm that identity we acquired in graduate socialization. One assumes in a remarkably brief time the culture of anthropology or sociology in graduate school. The culture and the identity that goes with it are central for the qualitative researcher, and so the field experiences are for the text. Life chances within a career are associated closely as a result of publishing books in genres that resemble, or at least address in a conforming way, the literature cited in the ones that preceded them. If you write a nonconforming text, then the rewards of the discipline may be withheld because the book does not read as a legitimated contribution to knowledge. Important for my argument is that written words and careers take place within an academy crosscut by disciplines — and both the academy and disciplines are market-sensitive corporations, the context of ethnographic text formation. Continental social theory in the lineage of Adam Smith, Marx, Weber, Durkheim, and (jumping to this side of the Atlantic) Parsons failed to account for the organization of Anglo-American society as a complex of corporate orders that includes absolutely critical social phenomena such as government, hospitals, and profit-making companies. The three corporate realms that dominate our cultural life in a legal-formal way are the public, nonprofit, and private sectors. Our universities and, interestingly, our trade associations (such as the American Sociological Association, American Folklore Society, American Studies Association, and American Anthropological Association) are all nonprofit corporations. Ethnographers are held firmly by the almost invisible bonds of the corporate world.

For me ethnography as a corporately configured way of life was broken open radically by the way I lived through fieldwork. Even crafting the text (stage 3) became an almost impossible task. As a result, I wonder about the form of life that ethnographers have cultivated since Malinowski. I join my voice with those who in growing numbers question the assumptions and practices of anthropology against the necessity to decolonize academic thought (Clifford, 1983; Clifford & Marcus, 1986; Dumont, 1986; Marcus & Cushman, 1982; Marcus & Fischer, 1986). When Clifford Geertz was awarded the National Book Critics Circle Award for Criticism in 1988 (Geertz, 1988), a larger social legitimacy was offered regarding the cultural scientist's concerns with culture and interpretation, inquiry and text, documentation and criticism. If Geertz raised the literary and interpretive possibilities within the endeavor, then Marcus and Cushman (1982) focused what a number of authors had been attempting in writing ethnography — to experiment until they had broken with the old categories and inaugurated a new narrative responsiveness to changing world cultural relations. Much of my recent work has benefited from the experimental moment, but is not derived from it. Both "Form of Life" and "Reversal" in this monograph have commonalities with a report entitled "Transformations of Disciplines Through Their Texts" (Rose, 1986) that amplifies points made on the socialization of anthropologists through their reading and its effect on ethnographic practice. In *Patterns of American Culture* (Rose, 1989), the pervasiveness of the corporation within the culture of Anglo-American capitalism is framed more broadly. *Patterns, Black American Street Life* (Rose, 1987), this book, and "Transformations" form a multiple set of inquiries that offer a working-out of the problem of conducting ethnography in America within the social forms that contain our lives and obscure to ourselves what we may indeed be doing.

It seems that when young ethnographers leave graduate school for the field there are thousands of possibilities that wait for them: The people will be hostile (as the Nuer quite justifiably were to Evans-Pritchard), or the people one lives among may delight in telling stories for the anthropologist's publicly announced book. On the other hand, despite the ever-different empirical realities of field stays, there has been a dominant mode of authentication for anthropological work: the ethnographic monograph or book. The genre has been stable for quite some time and its history, largely obfuscated, has existed longer than the academic discipline. To deal with the luxuriant diversity of human cultural life, anthropologists tended to standardize within a way of life, within the quotidian of the academy, with carefully conceived and highly monitored genres, the deeper identity of the writing and the experiences for the writing. Section 9 in this chapter exposes this point of view more fully. If the writing was not monolithic and was itself diverse, the diversity was controlled carefully, its boundaries visible to both readers and authors. The canon through this century has accumulated until we have between 8,000 and 10,000 scientific anthropological books about other cultures (not counting dissertations, travel accounts, anthologies, etc.), recognizable as such in anthropology libraries — a corpus that has as much as anything else defined a discipline, a way of knowing, a way of experiencing, indeed, a way of life.

It is as if we know by our texts and as if fieldwork is an extension of our anthropological, academic everyday life, a deformation of the outer skin of our western culture that never ruptures. In the field we are still academics, safe behind the membrane, we keep the same hours, do the same sorts of things, or do different things temporarily in order to advance our life chances back home. In brief, in the field we work. In the office we work. We work and we write.

1.

What relationships should ethnographers take up with peoples of other cultures or classes? Can we not move beyond abstract relations with them?

This question has been made more pressing by experimentation in the ethnographic text. The experimentation can be superficial unless the way of life on which ethnography is based is subjected to greater risks and thereby made more truly experimental. The text, of itself, cannot adequately break new ground. Ethnographers' lives, like the works they have written, have been standardized carefully at least since Malinowski: a summer in the field, two years in the field, subsequent summers in the field, and an occasional semester.

The hard questions facing ethnographers include: Is the one- or two-year field stay adequate to the demands of real cultural knowledge? Is any historically, textually ritualized formula for cultural knowledge adequate to its contemporary demands? In Chapter 2, it is urged that we take greater risks with our lives of inquiry and our relationships. New forms of cultural and social knowledge will surely be one of the results.

2.

We do not have an adequate understanding of our own culture of ethnographic inquiry — I mean an understanding beyond the confessional, self-observing pieces written in resistance to the hyperscience of 1960s cognitive anthropology. We do not understand ourselves as living within a culture of anthropologists, a subculture within university life. We do not talk about this in profoundly self-critical ways and that is why I would like to comment on the formation of ethnography as a way of living and a way of living differently — as a potent (sub)culture for conducting inquiry into culture.

3.

The ethnographers' interests narrow when there is exaggerated and exclusive concern with their own texts. One could examine only field notes, finally only field anecdotes, and so forth, working into smaller and smaller subsets of prose. At the same time anthropologists' horizons have expanded outward toward cultural and literary theory. It is the sacred activity of fieldwork that needs rethinking toward new forms of involvement. The idea of fieldwork demands not only critique but reformulation based on new relationships that we can take up across boundaries. New relationships across cultural lines imply profound changes in the culture of ethnographers (Hannerz, 1987).

4.

There is strong evidence that what we read affects directly what we perceive in the field. We know by our texts, we ask native women questions

18

concerning our anxieties as feminists, we examine subincision ceremonies as an exaggeration of our concern with our penises.

How do we break the narrowed cycle of conformity? How do we truly seek out and establish new modes of contact across cultures, through our lives, breaking with the received information in the books we have written and with our academic everyday life and the conventions of the academy?

5.

Ethnographers — like machinists, roofers, executives, and middle managers in corporate life — spend many of their waking hours laboring. The diffuseness of the tasks (such as committee work, talking with students, preparing to teach, faculty meetings, conducting research in the library, interviewing, or writing a paper to be read at the annual meetings) does not lessen its claim on our time or our thought. A number of academics stress that they always think about their work, and that the hours in their office are an indicator of their intellectual labors. We read and write, prepare and lecture inside legally incorporated bodies, institutions, and legal-rational organizations.

6.

By ethnography as a way of living, I paraphrase Wittgenstein, who would have called what we do *a form of life*. By it I mean that there are formal frameworks to our lives that contain them, such as corporations, of which we are all members. By corporations I mean the legally chartered public, private, and nonprofit institutions that are the scaffolding — or form — for our way of life in America. The corporations, as they have evolved, are (as Weber taught us) cultural formations as well as legal-rational ones. The corporations that make up Japan differ culturally in their history and foundations from Anglo-American ones, and the Anglo-American corporations are not at all identical with French, German, or Spanish companies.

7.

Ethnography, rather than retaining for itself some privileged place in Western thought, might well be examined as just one among a number of apertures that the West — mainly Anglo-American anthropology — has opened on other cultures. Rather than a hierarchy of methods of inquiry across cultures, we might democratically juxtapose ethnography with cultural journalism or ship captains' logs in order to see what conventions underlie observation and the making of texts of cultural differences consumed by the larger society, although I don't propose to do just that.

8.

To think about ethnographic texts and contexts, I want to examine some works from the late sixteenth and early seventeenth centuries, then read some documents from the first half of the nineteenth century. Against the background of failure of social thought to account for the culture of American corporations, I have read into the history of the formation of capitalist societies and cultures. In Foucault's *Archaeology of Knowledge* (1972) we are taught to look for discontinuities, strata that give way suddenly to subsequent occupations, disruptions in the record, and new discursive formations that displace older ones.

Despite the finding of breaks and fissures in the record around new formations — say, the abrupt disappearance of expedition anthropology and the establishment of academic anthropology at the turn of the twentieth century — continuities do remain, hidden from sight, often denied or obscured in the effort to legitimize the new order. I propose to read the continuities of concern in the following texts in order to claim that our interests and our institutional order, texts, and contexts have formed a tradition, albeit a constantly reobscured one that informs the present way of life of ethnographers. The texts I consult include Shakespeare's *The Merchant of Venice* and *The Tempest*. Two documents appeared between the performances of *The Merchant of Venice* (c. 1596) and *The Tempest* (c. 1613): The first document, which appeared in 1598, was the English translation of a book written in Dutch, *The Voyage of John Huygen van Linschoten to the East Indies*; the second, not a published book at all, was the letters and charters of the subscribers to the London Company of Merchants to the East Indies (1599 and after). The other readings include the *Report of the 1841 Meeting of the British Association for the Advancement of Science* (British Association for the Advancement of Science, 1841). This selection of documents helps show a continuity of corporate and intellectual form in the construction of what is now known as ethnography. The written text and the corporation evolved together in market culture, as did ethnography and the management of empire. By examining our history we find the hidden assumptions of our trade.

9.

Shakespeare's east-west geography stretched from the Bermudas to Greece, and those fictional terrains contrast interestingly with the economic and institutional developments through the last years of Elizabeth's reign. These fictional spaces were isomorphic with the rise both of capitalism and anthropology on the edges of the Atlantic, Indian, and Pacific oceans. His vision of the spatial extent of the economy was revealed in *The Merchant of Venice,* which depicted commercial transactions between friends and individuals known to one another. Just before Shakespeare wrote the play, the English maritime economy had been frustrated in the Mediterranean and, in competition with the Dutch, Portuguese, and Spanish, had begun to look to India and to the New World. The new route to India was not through the Mediterranean and then overland, but around the Cape of Good Hope.

On stage, Shakespeare's Bassanio asked to borrow interest-free money from a rich merchant friend, Antonio (the merchant of Venice), so that he might successfully court Portia, herself heiress to a great fortune. Bassanio would, if he married Portia, be able to reward Antonio's favor amply. Antonio, in keeping with a typical practice in the late sixteenth century, had his liquid capital tied up in ships that were even then sailing toward port. As a result, he felt forced to turn to Shylock for a loan with interest to grant his good friend Bassanio the necessary funds for courtship. In the person of Shylock, however, Shakespeare accurately perceived a worldwide trading network, far larger than the geographical setting of his plays. In his negotiations for lending the money Shylock, wise to the investments and vulnerabilities of Antonio's trade, tells Bassanio that

> my meaning, in saying he is a good man, is to have you understand me, that he is sufficient. Yet his means are in supposition: he hath an argosy bound to Tripolis, another to the Indies; I understand, moreover, upon the Rialto, he hath a third at Mexico, a fourth for England, and other ventures he hath squandered abroad.

The point here is that each loan was requested and granted by individuals who represented themselves or, perhaps in the case of Shylock or Antonio, family firms, but not corporations. It is worth emphasizing that from Mexico and the West to the Indies and the East, Shylock documented the space of early corporate capitalism and one of its informational sources, ethnography. In London, at this same time, there had been experimentation with the newer and non-kin-based joint stock companies where merchants would raise capital among themselves for joint ventures, usually for long-distance trade both East and West. This trade was the source, Braudel (1986) shows, of the rise of capitalism. Shakespeare could represent the economic flows between individuals, for individuals certainly lend themselves better to dramatic treatment than do institutions. But the then-current economic formations, indeed the rise of capitalism, lay in large part in firms that were based on neither friendship per se or kinship. I will develop this point more fully below.

Moving westward in Shakespeare's fictive space, *The Tempest,* located at the western geographical extreme, was a work that (although a romance) closely resembled what we now think of as science fantasy and scarcely alluded to money at all. The Duke of Milan, we learn, has been betrayed by his brother and deposed. Not killed, however, he and his three-year-old daughter were set adrift at sea and mercifully provided provisions. The desert island on which Prospero, the deposed Duke, finally landed was inhabited by an ugly monster, Caliban, who was in the fantasy of the time enslaved by magic and forced to do royal Prospero's bidding. Caliban's name may well have been a Shakespearian humorous anagram, a permutation of the word *cannibal.*

The New World—already dimly apperceived, perhaps, with the twin terms of savagery and slavery—was not portrayed by Shakespeare as the landscape of economic opportunity but of controlled irrationality and civilized judgment. The Europeans on the island were, through luck and magic, able to return to Europe, with wrongs righted between them, and Caliban—and even magic itself—left behind. Contrary to Shakespeare's vision of the New world (if that indeed is what it was) the northern littoral of North America was about to be colonized by England by means of a series of privately held companies, corporations designed to make fortunes for the investors. Nearly all the English colonies were established and managed by private concerns. Shakespeare had no way of foreseeing the developments, but I want to stress that the economy was moving from the Mediterranean to the world in new ways, particularly in corporate institutional formations and not in family firms.

Shakespeare's dramaturgical geography — classical, gothic, and fantasied savage — then simultaneously dramatized and contrasted with events in London that were pushing the North European movement of the economy away from the Mediterranean toward the western Atlantic and toward the longer, more arduous, and more remunerative voyages to the East Indies.

* * *

Shakespeare's career spanned the last years of Queen Elizabeth's reign and into King James's; *The Tempest* was performed in 1613 on the occasion of the marriage of King James' own daughter Elizabeth. No doubt many in the court had read Richard Hakluyt's *The Principall Navigations, Voiages and Discoveries of the English Nation,* first published in 1589 and enlarged and reissued between 1598 and 1600. Important as these works were for playgoers and businessmen, other books written at the time proved catalytic to the imagination of London merchants and to the making of new forms for raising and deploying capital.

Literary theorists remain marvelously silent on texts that tell us (or that we can tease into telling us) what to do. Fiction, on which literary theory practices most, does not in any direct sense point to the world and say, "You can do this." Fiction, except for the foolhardy, is not normative; its functions and felicities lie elsewhere. Other, nonfictional kinds of literature do construct sets of directions for operating significantly in the world. They are, in a sense, prescriptive. For example, much of the writing in the *Wall Street Journal* serves normatively for the investor. Travel accounts of the sixteenth century are another textual source where localities were transformed into consideration through writing such that those localities could be revisited, the second time for profitable trade. Description in the travel accounts had a declarative function and placed peoples, animals, localities, and goods in plain sight of the mercantile — the early capitalist — imagination (Buisine, 1981).

The adventurers — the merchants of Genoa, Amsterdam, or London — read several types of texts before they risked launching their ships with trade goods. In a sense, this is much the way ethnography is conducted: We read in order to guide the flow and type of field experiences. They, in their time, read in order to know where and what to trade.

In the years 1595 and 1596 two volumes were published that created a stir in Amsterdam (indeed, they were texts that launched ships), and in 1598 the English translation accomplished the same reaction in London. The volumes were John Huygen van Linschoten's *Itinerario*, a graphic account of his travels from Spain to India with the newly appointed Portuguese Archbishop of Goa. In form the book has interesting resonances with Malinowski's *Argonauts of the Western Pacific* (1961). Linschoten's introduction was a personal narrative, an "I was there" story-preface that tells of his childhood in Haarlem. The first sentence reveals that texts he had read preceded the documents he wrote, so that he was prepared beforehand to formulate his experiences as a voyager.

> Beeing young, [and living idlelye] in my native Countrie, sometimes applying my selfe to the reading of Histories, and straunge adventures, wherein I tooke no small delight, I found my minde so much addicted to see and travaille into strange Countries, thereby to seeke some adventure, that in the end to satisfie my selfe, I determined, and was fully resolved, for a time to leave my Native Countrie. (Linschoten, 1970)

Malinowski wrote within the frame of science while Linschoten employed the genre of *straunge adventures*. Linschoten did leave after reading and sailed for Spain where two of his brothers were living. One of them, a ship's purser, found a passage for him with the newly appointed Archbishop of Goa and in 1583, when he was 20, Linschoten sailed to the Indies. In 1592 he returned to Utrecht and — with the help of the physician, Bernard ten Broecke — wrote his *Itinerario* which, under Linschoten's patent, was published three years later together with pieces of other travel accounts and technical textual commentary written in by the doctor. The documentation was so powerful that the Dutch dispatched ships to India with Linschoten's volumes in the captain's cabin, and the merchants later formed the Dutch East India Company.

The account, which is not a gentlemanly travel account per se, is rather a complex documentary of tradable goods, ports, comments on the Portuguese amounting to intelligence reports, and observations of peoples and customs. There is a good bit of observation on the people inhabiting Goa and in chapter 33, for example ("Of the heathens, Indians and other strangers dwelling in Goa"), he noted the range of peoples there, funerary practices, dietary differences, beliefs, wedding ceremonies, witchcraft — but above all, with a very fine eye to material culture, sometimes described where goods could be found *by street*.

If one classified all he noted and described, it would encompass and exceed, perhaps, the *Notes and Queries on Anthropology* (Royal Anthropological Institute, 1951). At the same time, one could find resonances between his observations of place and those of a good ethnographer. I want to stress the continuities here of adventurers' and merchants' texts with ethnographic writing within the larger frame of a historic and continuing aperture by West Europeans on peoples of other cultures.

* * *

The effect in London of the translation of Linschoten's book was immediate. A number of well-to-do merchants agreed to form a joint stock company to lobby the Queen's Privy Council for a patent to trade in the East Indies.[1] On the 31st of December, 1600, a charter was granted to the London Company of Merchants to the East Indies (also known as the East India Company) with a monopoly for 15 years when it would expire and come up for renewal.

Thomas Smith, a leading London merchant who already had experience and some successes and frustrations with merchant companies, was appointed by Queen Elizabeth to be the first governor of the East India Company, but in the future the company was to elect their own governor from among their board of directors.[2] The charter, a legal document drawn up in Elizabethan prose (which reads like the legal documents of today) by the Privy Council,[3] established what became a board of directors and granted a monopoly of trade for Asia, Africa, and America with the caveat that the merchants would not trade with Christian princes in amity with the Queen. Those out of favor with the Queen, such as the Portuguese, were fair game for privateering, itself an activity legitimated through crown charters for which all ships at that time were well-armed. The merchants' patent or charter permitted them exemption from import duties on the first four voyages, and there were limits on the transactions in silver, the monetary metal of preference in India and the Spice Islands.

What I want to emphasize here is the power of writing that directs action — a kind of rhetoric that lets readers imagine what they can indeed do — its very immediate precedence over action, and the ways in which genres perpetuate themselves through successive generations of writers. The captain's journal, for example, was persuasive enough to warrant an iron-clad rule in the East India Company that

> every captain, master, master's mate, and purser should keep a journal which was to be handed in at the end of the voyage. That such accounts were put to a practical use in later voyages helps explain the fact that not more of them survived. (Strachan & Penrose, 1971, p. 13)

The Linschoten account was catalytic to the formation of a private corporation within a public corporation, the East India Company within the legal entity of the English Crown. The corporation was at that time a subject of change and experimentation, and at those early phases of capitalism had not yet coalesced into the modern corporation we associate with mid-nineteenth century capitalism to the present (Chandler, 1977).

* * *

In Shakespeare's *Merchant of Venice* we do not find an elaborate look into the interior of a business because commercial transactions were sublimated by the playwright to the interpersonal. With the rise of the English East India Company we can witness more than face-to-face intrigues. In the corporation there was both internal differentiation and external relationships. The corporation was dependent on an outside or higher authority for its own authority and legitimacy. Although the Queen as regency of a corporate body (the state) was believed, by herself and her subjects, to depend upon the dispensation of God, the state later acquired legitimate authority from the will of the people that was documented in a constitution for its supreme legitimacy. With the corporation one finds a legal license from the higher to the lower power, spelled out in writing, a document that charters the organization.

Inside the company there were officers, duly appointed and elected, who had to be legally and financially responsible and who were themselves governed by a board of directors. Power was slightly diffused in this way. The officers of the company had great powers in the Elizabethan company. The Crown transfered civil authorization over matters of justice to the incorporated merchants. In commissioning the first voyage of the newly formed East India Company, Queen Elizabeth sent an epistolary legal document to James Lancaster, captain of the departing fleet of ships. She wrote:

> & eury pson and psons ymployed vsed or shipped or weh shall be ymployed vsed or shipped in this voiadge in the said ffower shipps, or any of them, to giue all due obedience & respect vnto you, during the said voiadge, & to beare themselues one towardes another in all good order. . . . Wee doe heareby authorize you, to Chastice Correct & ponish all offenders, and transgressors in that behalfe according to the quallitie of their offence. (Birdwood & Foster, 1893, pp. 3-4)

This was a standard letter to captains of ships that indicates that the state franchised its voyagers with a legal privilege. Similar rules were written into the charter of the East India Company. The corporation had the power to make civil decisions over the men in their employ. Indeed, the powers were far reaching:

> ... being so assembled ... to make, ordain, and constitute such, and so many reasonable laws, constitutions, orders and ordinances, for the good government of the same company. (pp. 163-188)

Later the East India Company was granted the right to prosecute criminal offenses, and its power continued to broaden as it began to rule the Indian subcontinent. It is as if some powers of the state were transmitted and internalized inside the corporation, as if they had been standardized legally within an extended but corporately internalized civil polity.

The overall goal or mission of the authorized company was made explicit. The explicitness has been, up to the present, an integral part of a corporate charter or constitution.

The corporation, even in Elizabeth's day, required massive amounts of information from outside itself in order to operate. There are numerous examples in addition to Linschoten's of valuable information making its way into the knowledge of the directors of a company. In an anonymous book arguing for free trade and the abolition of the East India Company's monopoly, a historical note revealed the dependence of Queen Elizabeth's first ambassador to India, Sir Thomas Rowe, on the court of the Great Mogul. Sir Thomas learned — and it would not be difficult to imagine that he applied some diligence to it — which articles Europeans made that were most adapted for the India market:

> knives of all sorts; toys of the figures of beasts; rich velvets and satins ... wines of Alicant ... fine light armour ... large looking glasses ... French tweezer-cases; table books; perfumed gloves ... dogs of various natures ... and, in general any thing curious for workmanship, not at present known in India. (Anonymous, 1807)

The items seem exotic even today, but the point is that propitious acquisition of information made for the success not only of countries at that time but for the companies licensed by them.

We can identify here, I think, a *corporate principle,* a way of forming social institutions that although vastly changed has at the same time retained its overall recognizability as having continuity within Anglo-American culture. The corporate principle came increasingly, in northwestern Europe and in the United States of America later, to supplant the family and kinship as the fundamental motif for social organization. By corporate principle I mean a group of people who agree to form an organization legitimized by a higher authority but separate from it for agreed-upon purposes. The corporate principle, an incorporating principle, pulls the membership together by a text (its charter), a duly elected set of officers, a general membership, a budget, and some range of activities that members wish to pursue so as to alter some existing state of affairs. This bare-bones definition has been permutated in as many ways, probably, as there are corporations, but it was this evolving form of association that underlay capitalism and modernity as we know it. The noted political theorist Frederic Maitland (1958) observed, "for, when all is said, there seems to be a genus of which State and Corporation are species" (p. ix). When we look to the primitive world, anthropologists have told us that we can understand its organization through principles of kinship. If we look on the same grounds at the modern West, we find it organized as sets of nested corporations, and in the United States they are grouped into public, private, and nonprofit sectors. Indeed, under King James in the first year of his reign, it was proposed in the Privy Council that the New World be colonized as a public corporation by the Crown (a model followed by Spain). "The view did not prevail," as Griffiths (1974) explains, "and the matter was left to private enterprise licensed but not financed or organized by the state" (p. 141).

When we link together text and context we join Linschoten with the Dutch East India Company and to the London Company of Merchants. Writing, inscription, books, and knowledge were housed in gigantic corporate entities. Writing flows into, through and within, and to the outside of companies. Flows of information are stimulated and highly managed. The companies are built of paper and legal information on the social, material, and cultural worlds of importance to the companies.

A final coda on the English East India Company: the corporation was chartered entirely within the private sector as were the Hudson Bay Company and the Falklands Company but, like the somewhat similar English corporations that colonized America's northeastern seaboard, the East India Company began with its expanded civil charter to rule, to take over the function of the modern nation. In India, Brian Gardner (1971) wrote, the East India Company became a leviathan:

> A government which, through might of arms, was the most powerful in Asia; a government, the revenue of which was greater than that of Britain; a

government which ruled over more people than the present government of the United States; a government owned by businessmen, the shares of which were daily bought and sold. As Macaulay said, "It's strange, very strange." (p. 11)

There was enormous criticism of what the East India Company became on the part of Indian intellectuals and within England, notably by Adam Smith and Karl Marx. Finally, changing conditions brought it down. More powerful than the great dynastic families that preceded it, the London Company of Merchants transformed into the East India Company and existed from 1600 through 1813, when its monopoly was ended by Parliament. It then staggered on without its monopoly for 20 more years until it finally ceased operations.

* * *

I want to weave corporation and text together because in reality they cannot be sorted from one another. Ethnography as cultural practice will be foregrounded as a form of life within a social form, the corporation. The ethnographic book is a form of knowing and a more or less stable genre, but one that at the same time always changes. I begin in the past and move forward. In the report of the British Association for the Advancement of Science (1841), there was a committee report of the Natural History Section that had ties with the past that would affect the course of ethnographic inquiry over the next 150 years. Two years earlier a Dr. Pritchard had read a paper "On the Extinction of Some Varieties of the Human Race." He pointed out that science would suffer an irretrievable loss if a large portion of humanity counted by tribes were permitted to die out, uninvestigated. In response to his paper a committee was appointed to prepare a questionnaire for "Travellers and others" to carry with them on their journeys.

The appointed committee, reviewing other efforts at ethnographic inquiry, cited the *savans* of the Ethnographical Society of Paris who had printed a set of questions earlier; the committee found the French queries useful and freely appropriated them where relevant. The citation to the French contribution was perhaps not grudging but, like the competition between the English and Dutch merchants 200 years before, a real rivalry. This time the struggle was in the realm of science and was just as deeply felt. The committee wrote:

Britain, in her extensive colonial possessions and commerce, and in the number and intelligence of her naval officers, possesses unrivalled facilities for the elucidation of the whole subject; and it would be a stain on her character, as well as a loss to humanity, were she to allow herself to be left behind by other nations in this inquiry. (British Association for the Advancement of Science, 1841, p. 332)

The rhetoric was that of science — and one could almost sense a sacred quality to the word when it was used — but contained within a nationalist framework. Science was understood then, as it is today, as an instrument of a nation competing against other nations.

Although the queries of the committee were a far cry from Linschoten's observations, they may be seen as a continuing development and refinement — with borrowings from other sources — of an observational opening by the West on non-Western peoples. In 1841 the social formation that internalized the necessity for information was not a merchant company but what was to become after 1862 a not-for-profit corporation (by virtue of the English parliament's Companies Act of 1862) devoted to the advancement of science, the BAAS — in this case by the branch of natural history, an arm of investigation that included human natives, native vegetation, and native animals. Humans under the aegis of nineteenth-century science were naturalized like flora and fauna and their grid of specification was, like zoological phenomena, to be classified by race and language.

The imprimatur of the medical profession may well be seen on the form the queries took. The physical, which was coterminous with racial, came first. In the entire document there were 10 major headings and 89 numbered queries. One of the headings was a query without a number, so there were actually 90 general questions with unnumbered subquestions.

Within the queries such concerns remained as had been expressed during the Elizabethan voyages, colonization, and commercial relations. To be sure, newer interests were reflected, such as the hiring of laborers and the conduct of censuses. It is as if the categories of the queries were a fusion of science and the preoccupations of a corporate colonial power to whom textual knowledge was critical to its competitive edge and future successes. There was no precursor in the questions to a theory of culture that emerged in the modern period. The questions have a kind of uninspired pragmatic quality to them. The greatest curiosity, if we can judge by the length of the passages, was apparently aroused by physical differences and family life,

Table 1.1

Headings	Numbered questions	
Physical Characters	12	
Language	4	
Individual and Family Life	33	
Buildings and Monuments	3	
Works of Art	2	
Domestic Animals	1	(not numbered)
Government and Laws	13	
Geographic Statistics	7	
Social Relations	2	
Religion, Superstitions, etc.	13	
	90	

two concerns a physician might well find most important on a day-to-day basis. (See Table 1.1)

As the nineteenth century progressed, the queries of the natural history section of the BAAS gave way to *Notes and Queries on Anthropology,* a document first published in 1874 and revised and reissued in 1892, 1899, 1912, 1929, and 1951 (the sixth edition). Even as late as 1951, one can find textual affinities between the 1841 queries and the 1951 *Notes*, although between the two publication dates the academic discipline of social anthropology became highly developed. The publication of the 1951 *Notes and Queries on Anthropology,* revised by a committee set up by Section H of the BAAS, was organized as shown in Table 1.2 (Royal Anthropological Institute, 1951). I reassemble and juxtapose the 1841 queries next to the *Notes*.

The earlier queries had a category for domestic animals while concern with animals was distributed in *Notes and Queries* into the "Social Anthropology" and "Material Culture" sections. In the 1841 queries, the economy was absent as a numbered set of questions but still surfaced under such headings as "Works of Art." After asking for the particulars in artworks, the committee wrote, "Such particulars will not only throw light on the character and origin of the people, but will, directly or indirectly, influence the commercial relations which may be profitably entered into when commerce alone is looked into."

Throughout the 1841 queries there is a subtext of corporate capitalist interests manifest in reference to colonization, commerce, men who bear arms, and labor force potential. In the *Notes and Queries* of 1951 by

Table 1.2

Notes and Queries on Anthropology (1951)	*Queries Respecting the Human Race (1841)*
Part I Physical Anthropology	Physical Characters
Part II Social Anthropology	
I Introduction	
II Methods	Geographical Statistics
III Social Structure	Social Relations
IV Social Life of the Individual	Individual and Family Life
V Political Organization	Government and Laws
VI Economics	
VII Ritual and Belief	Religion, Superstition, & c
VIII Knowledge and Tradition	
IX Language	Language
Part III Material Culture	Buildings and Monuments
	Works of Art

contrast, a phenomenal preoccupation with social organization becomes apparent from the spatial orders of the household, settlement, and region to the kinship, economic, and political formations. The two texts are very different indeed, and I do not mean to attempt to reduce the disciplinary complexities of the 1951 *Notes and Queries* to the brief that travelers carried with them 110 years earlier. At the same time, the reader can find those deeper continuities that characterize cultural persistence at the most fundamental level (for example, the desire by corporate managers for systematic — even strategic — social knowledge written down).

* * *

On October 31, 1914, Bronislaw Malinowski (1967) wrote in his diary that he tried to synthesize his fieldwork results by reviewing the 1912 fourth edition of *Notes and Queries on Anthropology.* Later in *Argonauts* (Malinowski, 1961) he urged on others that same sort of manipulation of field notes while in the field, and in his own practices we can see the domination of the experience of the text. Text precedes experience, gives it shape; consciousness is informed continually by the literary material one has read. In Malinowski's diary entry we have the same relationship of precedence of text before field experience that we find in Linschoten's readings of *straunge adventures* prior to having his own adventures and then writing them up.

At the same time in Malinowski there is ample evidence that he carried with him his European context, which is nothing less than well-socialized behavior to corporate settings. A constant theme in the diaries is the effort to work, to make science, to sublimate pleasure — even leisure reading — to the intellectual labors at hand. Not only was text overlaid on daily life, gathering it up and regrouping it as written documentation, but the institutional behavior of an academic was clearly visible in the work load, the hours spent recording and participating for the sake of science itself.

By context I mean the tacit corporate context, the formation of the self around disciplined work and labor within an institution. Life in the organization entails being managed by others, the internalized management of oneself, the attitudes that one has acquired unconsciously toward the expectations of how one ought to comport oneself in the large firm (such as a university or profession). One of the best documented work loads of an ethnographer in the field, a corporate work site re-created in the field, is in Harold Conklin's (1964) brief log of a day (July 18, 1953). Although he offers in a note the caveat that no day is typical, he represents one almost as if it were the log in a highly controlled military mission: from "0600 I am awakened by the excited shouting of six Parina children who have found a neighbor's goat giving birth" to, at the close of the day, "2345 I spread out my mat. . . . But first 'Nonga' Balyan, and I discuss indirect manners of speech in Hanunoo" (pp. 119-125). The account was written originally as part of a report to the Social Sciences Research Council concerning his grant from them. The implied gigantism of a busy day as an ethnographer can be understood readily in this bureaucratic context where he had to justify the ways of ethnographers to man, even if it could not be believed to be an ordinary day.

I know of at least one anthropologist who believed that report of a July day to be no work of fiction but the ordinary energetic — and, to him, admirable — form of life Conklin led. From 0830 to 1200, 3.5 hours, Conklin wrote field notes and checked details of the previous evening with two eyewitnesses. The amount of work implied by the text, "A Day in Parina," portrayed a staggering quantity of ethnographic labor. It was almost like an academic's busiest day at the office.

Jeremy Boissevain worked just as hard, apparently. Sometimes he was able to squeeze in a short nap, but he was able not only to arise at 6:00 A.M. as Conklin had done, but to go from 15 to 45 minutes longer, until 12:00 or

12:30 A.M. (Boissevain, 1970). Most ethnographers do not log their days for us as Conklin and Boissevain did. Evans-Pritchard writes eloquently of the Nuer's opposition to his efforts to study them, but gives no graphic detail of an ordinary day spent with them (Evans-Pritchard, 1940).

* * *

I want to pursue the work habits of ethnographers who take their corporate settings with them in mind and in practice to the more remote geographies. For the most part anthropologists do not spend much time reporting on details concerning their everyday lives. We are given hints of what people do in the field. There is diversity, of course, and a great deal of continuity over time.

In 1943, while studying Italian-American men, William Foote Whyte got up at 9:00 A.M. in the morning, went to a restaurant for breakfast, and used the remainder of the morning to type his field notes of events from the evening before. He then ate lunch in a restaurant and set out for the street corner. He was back in the Martini household where he boarded for dinner with them, then back to the street corner for the evening. Apparently he went to bed around midnight (Whyte, 1955). Hortense Powdermaker (1966) discussed her day, and we catch a valuable glimpse of the dominion of writing in the course of an ethnographer's day: "Malinowski had also told us to note down everything we saw and heard, since in the beginning it is not possible to know what may or may not be significant. I faithfully tried to carry out this injunction" (p. 61). In 1963, Gerald Berreman (1972) wrote that he and his interpreter spent the first three months of his field stay keeping house and "attempting to establish rapport" under difficult circumstances (p. xxiii). Although one gains an impression from Powdermaker of the ethnographer with pencil in hand, one feels with Berreman the maddening frustration of not being able to work. Gerardo Reichel-Dolmatoff (1971) published in English an account of Amazonian cosmology based on work with a key informant, Antonio Guzman. "The investigator and the informant met during a six-month period for one to three hours daily in an office where, surrounded by books, maps, and photographs, our conversations developed without interrupting (sic) or distraction by others" (p. xviii). Robert Levy (1973) reported that he used psychological check sheets with informants, and we clearly see a text designed in advance that structures what both the anthropologist and the people from whom he or she elicits must do. Carol Stack (1974) also issued schedules but, as she explained, she and some of the people she lived with "together . . . worked out questions on various topics to ask the families studied" (pp. xvii-xviii). John Miller Chernoff (1979) revealed not so much the way a workday progressed—though he does convey that through much of the book—but how to enter other ways of life and participate at some level pretty much like one's fellows: "To arrive at the point where one sees the life of another culture as an alternative is to reach a fundamental notion of the humanistic perspective, and to accept the reality of one's actions to the people who live there is to understand that one has become part of their history" (pp. 9, 19-21). In 1979 a collection of papers on long-term fieldwork was published. The long duration of field engagement did not of itself alter the relations of anthropologists to those studied or the texts that served as models for the experiences and for writing them up (Foster, Scudder, Colson, & Kemper, 1979). Steven Feld (1982) recorded the variation of his days in the field, interviewing, transcribing, and taking musical recordings. Marjorie Shostak (1983) could, as had always been done by anthropologists, report on work with her major informants and her agenda for asking questions and directing conversations.

* * *

Anthony Seeger (1981) published a valuable portrait of a person who faced the agony of attempting to move by means of documentation an unincorporated way of life into a corporate one. I review briefly what he recounted in order to further the point that we carry our corporate cultures with us in highly formal ways when we do ethnography. I distrust those who admit to "letting the data" tell them what to do and think, because what they learned to let the data do represents only a marginal difference from structuring it as self-consciously as one can. Both the follow-your-nose and the rational, preplanned field styles rely upon a socialization to the same canonical features.

We can envision Anthony and Judy Seeger in their effort to impose a way of life on the Suya of Brazil's Matto Grosso, or finding accommodation between their way of life and the Suya's, or the Suya making an effort to accommodate the Seegers with their own best effort, or the Suya simultaneously resisting and aiding the Seegers. Whether we want to examine the cultural relation in terms of power (imposition), epistemology (mutual accommodation), or language (discourse, discursive relations) in which each constructed the other, we still have incommensurable forms of life interpenetrating with linguistic, authoritative, and epistemological conflicts and contradictions.

Rather than reduce my review of the Seegers' involvement in Suya life to a single factor, I prefer to examine it as forms of life in juxtaposition, as the uncertain double ground of inquiry.

Through Seeger's characterization of the field stay, we can observe the frustration of the corporate objective, its work ethic, and its self-defined rationalities. His rationalities, for example, were evidenced clearly when he wrote, "I terminated my fieldwork not because I believed I knew everything but because I thought I knew enough about those areas that interested me." It was systematic questioning, he explained, and careful listening that provided him with the information for his book. This systematic questioning was checked, he mentions, directly against the *Notes and Queries on Anthropology.*

Seeger's construction on the contact of the ethnographer's culture with Suya culture was that of frustration, the perceived continuing failure to achieve what a rationalized field method and doctoral dissertation proposal promised in advance of what he would find. During the first few months he reflected a common feeling among ethnographers: "I felt as though I was accomplishing nothing." Seeger had to hunt and fish to support Judy and himself, he had to get up early and treat peoples' illnesses, forage, and tend a garden eventually. His "informants" were either, he worried, hungry and hunting and fishing or full and sleeping. He did not unearth immediately the ritual information for which he was searching because it was the wrong season for ritual performance, it turned out in one case. In another, it was because people would not talk about it.

There was a raw contact zone between cultures: An academic resentfully had to hunt and fish; he had to learn the language without an instructor or times set aside for it by the Suya; the Seegers had to purvey gifts and medicine; they were recipients of stories and songs; the role, as he expressed it, of eavesdropper, gadfly, dependent, and manipulator of conversations became onerous. His dependency was overwhelming, and he wrote that he was operating as a Suya 12 year old when he left.

Although the bureaucratic norm of corporate academic life dominated his work expectations, it was the text he was planning to construct — the dissertation — that dominated much of that effort: "I always carried a small notebook with me and wrote down everything of interest. On long days of fishing I would think about what I had learned and write down questions to be asked. I would arrange questions into lists on a given topic. Equipped

36

with these general lists I would look for any person who could answer one of the various groups of questions." Through a haze of frustration — fishing, for example, while wishing to hear a story or ask a question — Seeger complained in a way wholly familiar to ethnographers. Although they lived in a large household of 35 people with whom they could sing for 15 hours at a time, and Judy could tell Anthony what the women were saying, the field experience was one of conflicting rationalities, physical sickness, and resistance to the Suya way of life even while trying to capture a priori chosen features of it.

The institutionally situated rationalities themselves lead to severe frustrations and, as well, to arbitrary involvement. Knowledge gathering and what is accumulated is itself highly arbitrary to fit into documentation recognized by peers as important within the traditional framework of the incorporated discipline. Seeger wrote that he chose to give himself five years to accomplish his work with the Suya and then turn to other societies and intellectual concerns. "This book," as he phrased it, "is an important step in that process."

* * *

I find it remarkable that in the relentless and what appeared to be the rather humorless efforts of the Seegers there was not some critical reflexivity, some questioning of the entire ethnographic enterprise. There was none, and it is remarkable for all that. The other ethnographers mentioned did not question the historically constituted relationships between cultures that ethnographic practice requires of its members. Indeed the ethnographic inquiry has been sancrosanct and left almost wholly uncriticized in its institutional standardization. It is the text that has received critical attention, not relationships across cultural boundaries. The level of internal criticism has tended to be, for example, conservatively made of models of particular cultures that are found wanting when applied to geographically remote cultures. We need to move beyond that kind of conservative, internal critique to ask the more fundamental questions directly of our observational practices.

As a result of severe depopulation, the cultural life of the Suya had been set irreversibly on a new course. Seeger lamented, "The material I was unable to obtain on social organization and defunct ceremonies was just what I had hoped to get from the Suya groups reported on the Arinos River in 1970." Why did he not begin to break with his carefully cultivated graduate student expectations and try to examine how people manage the contact directly or indirectly with an encroaching national and world civilization of which the Seegers were a part? Or, more to the point I am making, ask in a way that might affect ethnographers' practices, "What am I doing here?" I do not mean to reduce this larger question to a personal level. Really I am not asking the Seegers this question at all, but anthropologists.

The logic of inquiry, illustrated at the beginning of the essay, showed that first we read, then experience the world in the light of that reading, then publish the results of our reading and experiencing — in our case within the culture of American corporate life, the university, and profession. The question arises as to whether or not we can break the logic by taking up new relations within other cultures such that we begin to draft new forms of texts and explore new modes of experience. Maitland was critical of the corporations that England exported and with which it colonized. He went so far as to suggest that Englishmen were not well equipped to think about the challenges posed by Ireland, commonwealths, and corporations that had evolved since the sixteenth century under the Crown. The development of empire was neither anticipated by theory nor guided by traditional thought concerning the relations between state and corporate bodies. I am urging that within the larger scheme of things of the West, which continuously demands information on the rest of the world, that we consider the openings, such as ethnography, through which information flows. The boundary across which the information is gathered is a corporate one, and it keeps its edges rather sharply defined. Is it not possible to define the corporate boundary in new ways, to subvert it, to rethink relationships between ourselves and others? This is an issue that demands the attention of anthropologists to be sure. But other branches of learning and practice need also to rethink and anticipate what sorts of openings are desired between cultural orders and with what forms of relationships we might engage them. What new cultural formations and identities may suddenly arise?

2. REVERSAL

In the years 1969 through 1971 during the fieldwork stay, Telemachus, the man for whom I worked in the auto repair shop, commented to my wife about me. It was a cultural critique, a reading in reverse of the ethnographer, a reading through the eyes of one firmly positioned in his own everyday world. Telemachus Combs became, in a strong sense, the person whose advice I continually sought in the face of what was often a difficult, even hostile social world.

My wife at that time, Karen Rose, was back in the shop chatting with him. We lived right next door to his garage, and the two of them had formed a joking relationship. In the course of their conversation Telemachus commented to Karen, "Dan laughs and jokes but he never plays."

The comment was a deep one. Telemachus had a way of making condensed statements that, to those who could understand them, spoke worlds. Telemachus made a critique of the ethnographer as a sociable person, one who could joke and laugh at those who did but, significantly, did not play. *Play* was a complex, performed speech genre that the ethnographer, me, did not perceive at first and did not begin either to manage well or to perform until the second year of the field stay. The play was minor theater, a small dramaturgical mode of speech production that required several persons and an audience. Its basic form was the triad, where two performed before a third, or a generalized third. The difficulty in the play, for me, was in learning to improvise my lines to satisfy the fiction that was initiated by the first player.

What I want to emphasize is not the speech genre per se, but the implicit critique, the reversal of perspectives, the critique of the ethnographer by those for whom the ethnographer usually had provided the framing discourse.

To effect one kind of reversal is to hear, take up, discover, and legitimize the voices of other cultures against, with, or through one's own.

In the epigraphs that follow, each of the authors has suggested a reversed perspective to a received one — a critique of the West, a reading that runs counter to the hegemonic, the colonial, or the oppressive. The intention in quoting so many little excerpts is to focus, on the one hand, on how many scholars are interested in effecting and witnessing a transformation in point of view and to unfocus, on the other hand, until, through all the citations, we are launched outside our usual way of reading a text and its footnoting accompaniment to the prose constructed above.

The Epigraphs

The relations of power whereby one portion of humanity can select, value and collect the pure products of others need to be criticized and transformed. This is no small task. In the meantime, one can at least imagine [art] shows that feature the impure, "inauthentic" productions of past and present tribal life; exhibitions radically heterogeneous in their global mix of styles; exhibitions that locate themselves in specific multicultural junctures; exhibitions with nature in them that remains "unnatural"; exhibitions whose principles of incorporation are openly questionable. (Clifford, 1985, p. 177)

It is, then, the growth of science, not the 'subject' people (subject in both experimental and political senses of the word), that remains the anthropologists' paramount concern. (Diamond, 1980, p. 7)

For in fact we [Negroes] have rejected many of their [white] values from before there were Jim Crow laws. (Ellison, 1984, pp. 404-405)

I owe my teachers, the people of Ballymenone, honesty and accuracy. I let their creations stand as they shaped them, but I accept more than their words and the works of their hands. I begin my tale with their categories, with night and day, ceiling and farm, home, clay, moss, bog, talk, chat, and story, then push beyond, following their modes of reasoning to propose their world for contemplation within our own.

My responsibilities begin but do not end with my teachers. Ballymenone's people of the future will find here the texts they will need to understand their place, the texts they would have gathered themselves had they gotten the chance that I did. (Glassie, 1982, p. xiii)

The Jews, Horkheimer and Adorno argued, were prime targets of the totalitarian identity principle of instrumental rationality because they were the most resolute repository of otherness and difference in the Western world. (Jay, 1984, p. 39)

. . . a reversed polarity for anthropology which aims in the direction of a synthesis of center and periphery. (MacCannell & MacCannell, 1982, p. 70)

NARRATOR: Papua New Guinea. For most of us, an exotic-sounding paradise in the South Pacific, but for anthropologists, a unique laboratory for studies in human behavior. Yet how do those who live there feel about being the subjects of such studies. NOVA went to Papua New Guinea to find out . . .

NAHUA ROONEY: I think, in the '80s, we must stop anthropologists coming into the country. Secondly we have our own academics, we have our own Papua New Guineans who now can become anthropologists themselves. . . .

ONGKA (SINGING): "The sun rises up and then it goes down.
It won't be long before I die.
And there is one thing I would like to talk about.
People come here whom I don't know at all.

40

> *They come looking for Ongka.*
> *When they see me, they recognize me.*
> *My story goes out to the place of the white man.*
> *And while my story has gone there, I haven't gone*
>   *there myself.*
> *I haven't seen their places.*
> *I don't know what kind of planes they have there or*
>   *what kind of land they have there.*
> *Am I going to die without knowing their story?*
> *So that's the only thing I want you to know about.*"[4]
> (*NOVA*, 1983)

It is a new signifying process that alters the observer's perception of self and cultural other in such a way that the observer's *own* society is influenced and changed. . . . What I am referring to is a process of incorporation that is coded in a symbolic way that then alters the professional anthropologist's perception of self/cultural other, which *then* makes a different kind of impact on the professional's own society. (Prattis, 1985, pp. 266, 278)

I would wish to remind Saramakas who read or hear portions of this book to be sure not to treat it as a bible, but rather as an incomplete and early attempt to bring together the fragments of First-Time knowledge that I have been able to learn. It is intended, ultimately, as a celebration of the Saramaka historiographical tradition, as an example of how successful Saramakas have been collectively in preserving a vision of First-Time truths. And it is meant to encourage a whole new generation of Saramaka historians to continue the search and to broaden and deepen our understanding. (Price, 1983, p. 24)

Just as painters, according to Cezanne and Klee, should allow the universe to penetrate them, anthropological writers should allow the events of the field — be they extraordinary or mundane — to penetrate them. (Stoller, 1984, p. 110)

The esthetics of jazz demand that a musician play with complete originality, with an assertion of his own musical individuality. (Regardless of the public's acclaim for some noted imitators, musicians give only the meanest of rewards to camp followers). At the same time jazz requires that musicians be able to merge their unique voices in the totalizing, collective improvisations of polyphony and heterophany. The implications of this esthetic are profound and more than vaguely threatening, for no political system has yet been devised with social principles which regard maximal individualism within the framework of spontaneous egalitarian interaction. Then when Europeans and white Americans embrace the music, they also commit a political act of far more radical dimensions than that of espousing a new political ideology. (Szwed, 1980, p. 588)

Dennis Tedlock began a paper in just this way and effected a reversal on sociolinguistics by taking up a position inside the standpoint of an oral tradition. He turned the practices of oral performance back upon the written, the alphabetic tradition, forming thereby a critique of our literate legacy:

> I don't know where to begin this story. Quiché Maya stories occur naturally in conversation. People do not set aside an occasion for storytelling, where all other kinds of talk come to a stop. It is true that stories are likely to be heard at wakes, but people don't die just so someone can tell stories at wakes.
>
> A Quiché story does not begin with a series of formal opening announcements that call a halt to conversation and point only into the story, and it does not end with a series of formal closures that call a halt. The story may include or refer back to bits of the previous conversation, and when it is over, bits of the story are caught up in the conversation that follows. (Tedlock, 1983, p. 247-48)

> We, the non-elite, should resist the usual intellectual error that would have us find separate and different causes for the good and the bad sides of Western modernity. Its science and its politics, the successes and the failures, the internal and the external, all have the common quality, the unity that gives modern Western civilization its name and form. I wished to say that the spirit and the form of the whole history that culminated in the horrors of Auschwitz and Hiroshima, fascism at home and imperialism abroad, depended upon that structure of science and politics, philosophy and technique, whose foundations had stood divided by mutual reciprocal consent for several centuries past. (Uberoi, 1978, p. 84)

> If "culture" becomes paradoxical and challenging when applied to the meanings of tribal societies, we might speculate as to whether a "reverse anthropology" is possible, literalizing the metaphors of modern industrial civilization from the standpoint of tribal society. . . . Our discussion has shown that there is no reason to treat cargo cult as anything but an interpretive counterpart of anthropology itself, and that its creativity need not be any more problematic than that of the anthropologists who study it. (Wagner, 1975, pp. 31, 34)

Phenomena

The epigraphs for the most part converge on a critique of Western discourse about diverse cultural streams. Although not all the people quoted wish to effect as full a reversal as would, say, Prattis, Tedlock, Uberoi, or Wagner, the groundwork has been prepared to begin effecting reversals on received cultural practices and thought. Ethnographic poetics and fiction seek to move in the same direction. A reversal sets up a self-conscious counter-discourse and erodes the hegemonic position of the ideology of cultural purity and racist exclusion.

The phenomenon of reversal is everywhere around us, particularly in the mass media, television — such as the *NOVA* show quoted briefly in the epigraphs — and in newspaper articles:

> These days the talk is of Emaneya Mubiala and his group, Victoria Eleison, who hit the stage of one of the nightclubs three nights a week. The next generation of Zairian music, they say, is happening at this club.
>
> "I'm modernizing Zairian music," said Emaneya, as he is known across Zaire, leaning back into the deep cushions of a velveteen sofa in his house in the Cité. "I make it more appealing to the young by making the music progress a little bit, by adapting from American music a little." (Gargan, 1986)

In a feature article entitled, "Through a Soviet Lens: Gomorrah on Hudson," Philip Taubman (1986) of the *New York Times* reported on a Soviet documentary of America and New York City. He wrote that the film "portrayed New York as a modern Gomorrah, focusing on the misery of the homeless, the squalor of Times Square and the presence of prostitution, drug addiction, pornography and poverty." Here the specular image of ourselves by a rival culture is held up to us through a feature article, not the documentary film the Russians made. There is here a mediated reversal muted by reporting rather than a direct viewing. The critique of our society by theirs which by reading we may internalize has an implicit, almost oneiric, quality.

Such reversals, mediated by writing but less critical, have been going on for some time. When in 1902 Sir Apolo Kagwa journeyed to London from Uganda to witness the coronation of King Edward VII, he left, through his secretary, an ethnographic account of his travels in England. In a chapter on his observations entitled "The Stomach of England," his secretary recorded:

> We saw, too, where they forged gun-barrels, and also a hammer as large and as high as a hill made by white ants. Do not think that men hold these hammers and work with them; this is not so at all. In England a great deal is done by hand, but it is usually the case in the country. In great factories machinery is their servant; and their wisdom and strength are put into these machines, so that they become like human beings to work by themselves. . . .

The whole works were as large or larger than the space in front of the King's enclosure in Mengo, and there are twelve thousand men employed in them, and they come from every part of the country and keep changing. (Mukasa, 1975, pp. 110-112)

The relationship between the English gathering data and the Africans gathering data continues, but with surprises and new twists, amazing reversals. When Mswati III was crowned King of Swaziland a crisis in knowledge occurred because the last coronation had occurred in 1921. Michael Parks (1986) of the *Los Angeles Times* wrote that

so few people remembered Sobhuza's installation as king in 1921 that Swazi officials, to their embarrassment, had to ask Britain, the colonial power here at the time, to search its records for accounts of the secret rituals and ceremonies then. To aid future generations, most of the ceremonies were videotaped this time.

To reverse the reversal, not only do the musicians of Zaire and nearly everywhere else import influences, American musicians become the students of performers in other cultures—including sometimes those who already had built in Western styles. Robert Palmer (1979), in writing the liner notes for Philip Glass and Robert Wilson's *Einstein on the Beach,* explained,

What's happening is an important shift in the way Western concert music is composed, performed and appreciated. . . . Glass was studying with Allah Rakha, the Indian virtuoso of the tabla drums. Through this association he became involved with the Indian sitarist, Ravi Shankar, who hired him to help in the scoring of a film. "My ideas wouldn't have developed the way they did if I hadn't started in that place," Glass says. "Also, I travelled in Morocco, where I had my first contact with non-Western music and was influenced by the geometric repetitions in Islamic art. Then in Asia I would stay in Himalayan villages for two or three weeks without seeing another Westerner. Later I became interested in South Indian music and in West African drumming."

What I am suggesting is that the cultural reversals that we witness everywhere around us are not unique to ethnographers, although ethnographers do tend to be more intensive in scholarly pursuit than the interplay of influences I've documented.

What is possible in this space of contact, crossing over, assimilation, appropriation, juxtaposition, and fusion has not been adequately explored; indeed, this space has no real name. What we know is that there are numerous ragged zones of contact between peoples who hold incommensurable values and beliefs, traditions, and philosophies.

Although anthropologists have borrowed from the linguists the term *creole* to account for what goes on in this space, I want to talk more about reversing, less about language formation and more about what goes on there, rather than use a linguistic term as a metaphor for the explosion we witness of processes and practices in cultural collisions. Actual cultural movement today is more like competition and appropriation and the continuous formation of new cultural possibilities than the term *creole* suggests. It is the discursive space where multiple voices sound from vastly different cultural traditions on which I want to focus, although the focus will be narrowed to a few poems.

Relevance

The central question is where ethnographic poetics is located and what is possible for it. As to location, ethnographic poetics inhabits an outlying village at the edge of the metropolis of cultural theory. I am thinking of the cultural theory that shapes contemporary consciousness, that informs the various academic factions and is fed continuously by them. Cultural theory since World War II was framed for the Anglophonic world by Eliot and linked to religious civilization. For literary theory and many of the readers of cultural theory the conservative branch of cultural studies to which Eliot and others gave voice was pushed aside by the critical thought of the members of the Frankfurt School (which had its sources in prewar Germany), the French, and the English Left, notably Raymond Williams.

Various academic branches draw from critical theory to address questions generated internally by the several disciplines. Comparative literature, gender studies, folklore, literary theory, art theory, English, anthropology, Romance languages, Slavic studies, and political economy now take up critical positions and make critical readings of discipline-relevant phenomena.

At the same time that cultural theory has achieved unquestioned success in addressing the current crisis of representation in the cultural sciences, the figures that we associate with it — Benjamin, Bourdieu, Foucault, the Frankfurt School, Levi-Strauss, Lyotard, to name a few — failed to establish human cultural *diversity* at the center of concern. One is hard-pressed to find cultural differences at the heart of discussion, whether in Williams or Foucault.

In drawing from Continental cultural theory ethnographers have wished to address the crippling weakness. Marcus and Fischer (1986), in their effort to redress the absence of cultural diversities within the body of cultural theory, find that there has been a widespread crisis in representation. In anthropology, they acknowledge the erosion of what they term "base concepts" such as social structure or the primitive. This crisis of representation affects most of the social sciences and challenges, by considering science itself as textual codes to be interpreted, the positivist system of thought that has held sway over the past 40 years.

The crumbling of the older representational forms has fueled experimentation in anthropology notably in the writing of ethnographic texts, arguably its most distinguishing internal practice. To meet the challenge, Marcus and Fischer tell us, we ought to inaugurate and systematize cultural criticism, at the heart of cultural anthropology. This collective pursuit of critique is to be based firmly within ethnography whereby the ethnography that an anthropologist writes must critique explicitly the rapidly progressing homogenization of world culture that lies implicit within the view of the people the ethnographer studies. In a sense this constitutes a reversal, but a narrow one. They propose that the unifying task of a reconstituted ethnography is to be continually reactive and critical. There is no exploration involved, and more to the point, they do not demonstrate that the future of ethnography and anthropology lies in part in the establishment of new relationships across cultural and class boundaries. It is not in criticism but in relationships, whether dialogical or miscegenating, that the promise of the field resides. There is much to recommend their proposal, but it is hardly definitive of what we can or want to do.

An ethnographic poetics desires more, indeed nothing less than to inhabit a zone of contact (by crossing over it again and again) which cannot be defined but must be explored, which can take its shape through ethnography, poetry, fiction, and the other arts (the ethnographic art of Lothar Baumgarten is particularly relevant). A literary ethnography may well go beyond critique to celebrate differences or the fusion that results from differences that have been historically worked out to make of traditional differences something new. By attaching ethnography to cultural theory that needs doing, there is the danger that the opportunity for more profound exploration in ethnographic field practice will give way to the real possibilities of superficial involvements that historically have plagued both journalism and criticism.

There needs to be a caveat here. Although I will advance an anthropological poetic as a vanguard of the new democratized epistemology and have stressed relationships across boundaries as more important than methodology per se, it is not the poetic for itself that I discuss it. The aim is to urge the engagement across social and cultural edges, to break frames, disciplinary rules, received notions, and the conventions of fieldwork with its repetitious intellectual labors. My purpose in reading the poetic of cultures in contact is the result of finding there a nonhierarchical approach to knowledge, a refreshing directness of experience between one segment of humanity and another.

The Poetic Voices

The poets are effecting reversals through their voices they take up in the poems. Michael Cook—a Newfoundland poet and playwright who, he tells us, was "born of Anglo-Irish parents"—starts a poem by taking on the imaginatively reconstructed voice of Nonasabasut, Chief of the Beothucks. The whole poem becomes a chiefly dramatic monologue. But Nonasabasut was the *last* chief of the Beothucks and in Cook's (1979, p. 4) poem sadly addressed the whites and lamented the passing of his people.

> Do not keep us alive
> in the minds of men,
> or let their dreams
> arrest our journey.
> It was a good destiny
> I have learned,
> we walking in sleep
> not to wake in the New World,
> and those grim men . . .
> became our saviours
> and the inheritors of our suffering.
> For we were what we were
> and nothing changed us
> from our coming to our going.

Stanley Diamond, our finest anthropological poet, uses the same first-person voice with animals and native peoples to effect a poetic and implicit political reversal. In "Return to the River" (1985), he writes as "Otter is speaking" that he is "dying in my own river/My estranged river" (p. 17), and continues through the imagined voices of the mythical animals of bear and turtle to an Indian voice—again, like Cook, talking for another within a different culture than the poet's:

> Oh MAHECANTTIU
> River they call the Hudson
> Curving like the body of our mother
> Gathering rain
> Black under black cloud
> Red under dying sun
> Oh river that flows through the dreamtime (p. 26)

This long poem closes with the words of a white European ("First White Man"), but we no longer have the verse that Diamond associated with Indian utterances; we have prose. Diamond began with the mythical animals, then progressed through the Indian voice, then overlaid the European voice— prose over poetry, domination over a once quasi-autonomous traditional culture. The reversal is effected by the first-person plural but also makes an explicit critique of culture through the device of voicing.

The American anthropologist or poet who poetically invents the speech of another attempts to recombine identities through an imaginative literary reconstruction or construction. At the same time that this poetic is brought to life, the voices of that other place and the people living there now already exist, have existed, and increasingly they have access to the same publications as the white who is writing over, or, in a sense, voicing over theirs (Prattis, 1985).

Rosario Morales (1985), who identifies herself as "a New York Puerto Rican," writes in a poem entitled "I Am the Reasonable One" how reasonable she is to members of the white culture. Then at the end the prose poem turns abruptly to its contradiction:

> And I am angry, I will shout at you if you ask your venomous questions now, I will call you racist pig, I will refuse your friendship.
>
> I will be loud and vulgar and angry and me. So change your ways or shut your racist mouths. Use your liberal rationality to unlearn your contempt for me and my people or shut your racist mouths.
>
> I am not going to eat myself up inside anymore. I am not going to eat

myself up inside anymore. I am not going to eat myself up inside anymore.
I am going to eat you. (p. 202)

I am indicating here that this contact region between cultures does not
rely wholly for its voicing on ethnographers or whites crossing over. Though
geographically distant, a similar angry voice can be heard (though more
muted and poetic) in the writing of the Greenland Inuk, Aqqaluk Lynge
(1985):

You import illnesses
and give us a hospital

or

Today
the sorrow hit us
Thousands of years of suffering
hidden in our ancestor's proud hospitality,
hidden in our generation's frustration
were suddenly cut open
just today
and flowed out
and out

We have paid with our lives and our bodies
We have cried in protest

our cries have been heard
but have been put in abeyance by a bureaucracy of
        impotence (pp. 247-251)

Contradictions and collisions occur when a Western author writes about a
people who can also write about themselves. If this does not pose a crisis for
anthropological poetics, it certainly raises an issue of competing perspectives and sensibilities in a space of conflict between cultures. If I were to
write a poem as if I were black, after having lived with blacks for some
years, what sort of response would I receive from established and distin-
guished black poets? This is a heavily freighted question, but is no different
as I frame it here than if one would write a poem about Eskimos and contrast
it with poems that Eskimos now write. Fortunately we can examine the

contrastive texts of anthropological poets and Eskimo poets and ask what we find there. We may contrast Diamond's fine poem "Eskimo," and the work of Lynge, which we have in translation. The first lines of Diamond's (1982) poem are:

Eskimo
self-conceived animal

haloed
in fur of white fox
stands
at the center of night
dismissing
silence upon silence
stars drop
the temperature of ice (p. 51)

And divergently for Lynge (1985):

Among the eternally travelling eskimos
there was no need to settle down
in one special place
But when the whites came and
found they could draw money from the ground
they built a mining town
and summoned the eternally travelling humans
before them

The old bearhunter
was among them
whom we met in the now abandoned mining town
. . . manpower superfluous
. . . re-socialization a failure

. . . four fish/per day/per person
. . . pro persona
. . . hunting conditions not ideal
They pushed us away from our life
and now they hunt us. . . .

Soon I'll be used up (p. 248)

The reversal, the space of discourse and counterdiscourse, is a political space in which voices are raised that remain incommensurable; they do not map to one another, they do not share the same sensibilities. Indeed, they do not share the same historical moment. The Eskimo of today has evolved from the time of the ethnographer, which is fixed in the time of tradition as it is imagined to have been by the poet. The voice of the ethnographer-poet sounds slightly arch in contrast with the contemporary Eskimo poetry. This is an important realization and should not be elided. We should face our emotional responses to the way the readings feel juxtaposed with one another. How do we discover that Diamond's "Eskimo" sounds arch, and how do we become alienated from a fine piece of work?

Our uneasiness arises by being confronted with one of the wounded and accusing verses of the people about whom Diamond has written. The Eskimo, too, writes and talks, and his poem neither reflects nor parallels that of the white poet. Our alienation arises through a poem written from outside that penetrates us from outside, that strikes us with its vision of the world — its suffering inflicted on them not by us directly as persons but by our way of life, of forces outside ourselves or Aqqaluk Lynge. But the poem is aimed, nevertheless, at we who read it. Thrown toward us, wounding.

We are caught up in an inadvertent reversal, alienated from ourselves, and at the same time kept within our own cultural perimeters. We are unable to run, unable to become the other even while distanced from ourselves, unable to hide from the others, and having to confront others who are different and who resist who we thought they might be. Lynge is an elected official, and his poetry, even if he were not a politician, would create a political space, all the more so juxtaposed with Diamond's. The zone of cultures at their edges and penetrations (by means of the translation and printing inside a book, inside a poem) is resistant and difficult, apposite, and at the same time the source of suffering and renewal.

The space that is opened by our contacts, by the propulsion of our media and our global search for minerals and markets contains all the possibility for reversal, for taking up others and being taken up by them. This poetic, discursive, romanticized, angry space has not been named. I urge that we become more self-conscious of it, that we concentrate on it, that we do more work there. The great challenge for us lies in what we are making in the interstitial cultural zones that are neither wholly here nor wholly there.

Going back and forth across the nameless space of vital contact is possible, and a new democracy of theory for this zone has been urged on us. Uberoi (1978) writes: "By way of permanent solution, I think that there is nothing for it but to lift our false limitation and admit all theories, native and Western, new and old, classical and vernacular, to fresh scrutiny and independent judgment, for or against, in the light of the relevant facts" (p. 15). This has begun to happen in contemporary ethnography, where Western ideas are used to elicit but not to dominate the ideas and practices of the peoples Westerners study.

In the English language, creative leadership in the literature of cultures does not reside in the ethnographer-poet or translator. There has been an eruption of sensibilities across the planet that no intellectual field yet formulates in terms made expressly for academic understanding. I am referring to postcolonial literature, the *new literature,* or world literature in English. It is this literary stream to which ethnographic writing must attach itself in order to find sources of inspiration and to achieve its own most sophisticated contribution. From the Antipodes and the Pacific Basin, Africa, the Caribbean, the Native American and black American writers have passed far beyond ethnopoetics, translations, ethnographic fictions, and ethnographies. At the same time, in the contested space of our language, our cultural poetry and fiction, there are endlessly new jointures of literary sensibilities and cultural possibilities. Indeed within the conflict and blendings across world cultures, ethnographer-poets or writers and literary figures (whether Maori or Nigerian or North American) have begun to explore the same explosive processes — processes of cultural resistance, formation of new identities, rural-urban dichotomies, efforts to join the international market and equal efforts to reshape its incursions, and so forth. Diamond and Lynge, and the other players, demonstrate the deeply felt issues and the human aesthetic potential inherent in the space now opened to cultural reversals. There are new literary connections to be made for both ethnographers and poets.

World writers in English and in translation to English appear in numerous journals and books published in America and England. To our delight, ethnographers have been represented in these pages as well. A sampling of magazines, journals and books include: *Antaeus, Chelsea* (especially #46), *Conjunctions* (see Barbara Tedlock's stories in #9 and #13), *Critical Inquiry* (especially Volumes 12:1 and 13:1), *Grand Street, Granta, Harper's Anthology of 20th Century Native American Poetry, The Paris Review* (especially Ben Okri's story in #105), *Tri-Quarterly,* and *Zyzzyva.*

Reverie

He began to think about the unnamed space and crossing it to another cultural side and returning to the original location that had already shifted from the time he left. He imagined that he would make certain choices that would affect, from the moment they were made, the possibilities of the text, of any poetics, of anything he would write about others.

He left alone for a year to conduct ethnographic inquiry among the Ladas. When he arrived, they built a house, and he lived among them, although he was considered to be alternately immature or dangerous because he lived alone. . . . or,

He left alone, hoping for an uninterrupted year of ethnographic work, but found on arriving that he was incorporated relatively soon into an extended family. He become engaged to a woman and her family made plans for their marriage. Before the wedding he left to talk with his professors at graduate school about extending the time he expected to complete the dissertation. He returned and was married. He finished the dissertation in the field and by mail scheduled a defense of the work. The dissertation was accepted and he returned to the field and to his wife who was expecting a child. In the field he wrote articles and applied for teaching positions. His first interview was ten thousand miles away. He worked out a relationship with the university that paid him for four months there, but the understanding was that he would be living with his family among the Ladas the rest of each year. Over the years he began to explore the life of the Ladas from many sides and his understanding deepened as his family grew and aged. Each year he travelled to the university and taught for four months. As the years went by he was continuously asked by the Ladas to explain himself and why he had lived among them and what life was like that he left behind. He began to write down stories of his childhood and to explain the customs of the country where he grew up. He read the stories to his relatives and friends.

He spent longer times researching certain aspects of politics and especially literature of his country when he was at the university and began to extend his stay each year. Sometimes he took his wife and children and they lived near the university and continued after the end of the semester to examine the culture of the country and turn the inquiry into stories that he then wrote in Lada on returning home.

At the university people become more and more interested in the life of the Ladas that he had written about over the years and wished to know more. He was asked to deliver papers, write chapters in books, and authored ac-

counts. He hurried back to the Ladas at the end of the semester and began to spend less time around the university. . . .

* * *

The space of discourse that we have not named contains the edges of incommensurable cultures.

The space contains incommensurable, untranslatable emotions, beliefs, and aesthetic sensibilities.

It is a space of appropriation, borrowing, and juxtaposition

> of critique
> of resistance
> of creative collision
> of people continuously born into neither one side nor the other.

It is a space of the subversion of self-privileging positions.

It is the space of the formation of new sensibilities.

It is the space of making

> new literatures
> new experimentations
> new collaborations
> new performances
> new aesthetics
> new inquiries
> new hostilities, revitalizations, pieties, and revivals.

It is a space of interpersonal contact, of humor and joking relationships, of unconscious apprenticeship and assimilation, of parody, embarrassment, and ridicule (see also Said, 1989, p. 225).

* * *

His daughter who was half American and half Lada, though as he looked at her, it was difficult to find physical proportions of perfect fractions associated with either cultural identity, talked with him after dinner one evening not long ago. He was sitting in the front of the house watching the fading of the light and she came up and sat with him. Without much preamble she announced to him,

"Papa, I have decided to become an anthropologist."

He knew she was a person who closely observed other people and who seemed to have from childhood an inordinate curiosity about the lives of people, unlike the other children. Nevertheless he was surprised.

"Why?" he asked her.

"Because," she replied, growing more thoughtful and serious than she had been at first, "there seems to be two things happening at once in the world. Peoples imagine themselves to be distinctive, set apart from all others, exclusive, even specially chosen by gods or fates. At the same time other peoples imagine themselves to be a part of a larger humanity, to be universal, to be or act for all humans. It's as if we were continuously being split apart into cultures turned inward, and joined into larger formations that seek to embrace us all."

"And where do you fit into all of this?" he wanted to know.

"I don't know," she answered, "but I want to find out, because I believe myself to live neither in a small world imagined to be the one chosen humanity, nor to master the illusion that I am a member of some all-embracing, self-conscious world. I think that most of all I am in motion and that I am looking at the same time for who we humans can become and who I want to be."

He did not know what to say at first and they fell into silence. In the gathering darkness he thought back on his own youth and wished he had begun with such an awareness as hers to pull him forward into itself.

Full darkness finally concealed them from one another's vision; only their voices identified that they were still there. He broke the silence to encourage her not so much on the search, but on what she must do to make something significant of what she found. He urged her to establish new cultural relationships and then to write about them.

* * *

After nearly six years of continuous fieldwork among the Yanomami, Jacques Lizot (1985) wrote a book while still there. He explained in the English preface to it:

> I am not yet ready to speak of the terrible shock that this experience was for me, nor of the price I had to pay to become closely acquainted with a civilization so radically different from my own; perhaps I will never be able to speak of these experiences, for I would have to evoke so many harrowing

things that touch my inner being. There is a wound that first must heal.
(p. xiv)

But turning this statement around it is obvious that peoples dealing with much of the West, including individuals such as Aqqaluk Lynge, also feel the way ethnographers such as Lizot now realize from within. This response across cultures, especially those remote from one another, exists everywhere in the world and is, perhaps, a major contemporary emotion, and spreading.

What we do not command at this point is a mode of discourse that is culture- or value-free. When we write about other cultures that is itself a political act, or when we perform the music of others who also perform our music. These politics of narrative and of poetics admit of no transcendence. Self-privileging incurs serious moral cost, for it reduces the potentiality of the aesthetics of discourse across cultures and within the new space where reversals occur, now fundamental to the possibilities of a human poetic and an interhuman inquiry. Indeed, the most radical position that we can take — and take it we must — is to imagine the democracy of this new aesthetic space where cultural voices reach across to one another and where they contend and converse.

3. NARRATIVE LIVES

The claim that we know by our texts with which the book began, and the urge to break through our corporately framed lives by courting reversal of perspective through acquiring other ways of life as ethnographers, now come full circle, back to the books — and by implication other genres — in which we now write. We are witnessing a momentous reconfiguration of the cultural sciences, and I want to address briefly and in somewhat condensed, manifesto-like manner the new textual formation. It is ultimately, however, the interior, re-evolving relation between texts and lives that is of moment, but, in concluding, the emphasis will be suggestive of method and directions for future authorship and what this implies for our lives in the departmental-ized university.

Over the past 20 years there has been a sea change in ethnographic practices that has attended the rise of a number of cultural shifts. Respond-ing to these, George Marcus (1982) named the revolution of the writing of ethnography *the experimental moment,* and focused on ethnographies as texts (i.e., on the rhetorical construction of ethnographic writing and reading

56

and what about it was changing). That transformation of experimentation and concern with writing is now in its first phase, complete; we have a growing number of narrative ethnographies, and those written since 1985 include John Dorst's *The Written Suburb* (1989), Michael Jackson's *Barawa* (1986), Kirin Narayan's *Storytellers, Saints, and Scoundrels* (1989), Robin Ridington's *Trail to Heaven* (1988), Dan Rose's *Black American Street Life* (1987) and *Patterns of American Culture* (1989), and Paul Stoller's *In Sorcery's Shadow* (Stoller & Olkes, 1987) and *Fusion of the Worlds* (Stoller, 1989a).

In each of these volumes there is a longer or shorter temporal unfolding in the narrative; the author is an integral part of the action.

Borrowing from Bakhtin's theoretical observations (1981), one can observe that the novel has invaded the scientific monograph and transformed it — not through the use of fiction particularly, but through the descriptive setting of the scene, the narration of the local peoples' own stories, the use of dialogue, the privileging of the objects of inquiry along with the subject or author who writes, and the notation by the author of emotions, subjective reactions, and involvement in ongoing activities.

Bakhtin shows that the novel includes a multilayered consciousness, radical temporal coordinates, and maximal contact with the present. These features are becoming used more readily in the narrative ethnography. The future of ethnography lies in a more sophisticated and self-conscious relationship with the novel, that is, with the possibilities of social inquiry that the novel (itself an experimental form) has opened to us.

One of the great achievements of the twentieth century is Hermann Broch's *The Sleepwalkers* (1932/1964). It is a multigenre or polyphonic novel dominated by a single theme, that of the loss of cultural values. The theme is manifest at two levels: (1) in the lives of the characters who live between its covers, and (2) in the multiple genres used by Broch to convey narrative, poetically induced feeling, and idea.

The Sleepwalkers begins with and contains a kind of nineteenth-century realist narrative, but subverts itself halfway through by using such genre elements as the reflective and critical philosophical essay, lyrical poem, legal contract, stream-of-consciousness poetic, and excerpted newspaper article.

I would argue that the future of ethnography — whether in sociology, anthropology, psychology, critical legal studies, planning, or folklore — will be a polyphonic, heteroglossic, multigenre construction and will include:

(1) the author's voice and own emotional reactions

(2) critical, theoretical, humanist mini-essays that take up and advance the particular literature or subliterature of the human sciences and particular disciplines (perhaps an ethnography will develop one or two ideas that provide coherence to the entire book)

(3) the conversations, voices, attitudes, visual genres, gestures, reactions, and concerns of daily life of the people with whom the author participates, observes, and lives will take form as a narrative and discourse in the text— *there will be a story line*

(4) poetics will also join the prose

(5) pictures, photos, and drawings will take up a new, more interior relation to the text—not to illustrate it, but to document in their own way what words do in their own way

(6) the junctures between analytic, fictive, poetic, narrative, and critical genres will be marked clearly in the text but will cohabit the same volume

Multigenre fiction and poetry have been present in America throughout the modern period in such experimental forms as William Carlos Williams's *Paterson*. Milan Kundera discusses the European version of polyphonic novels in his book of essays, *The Art of the Novel* (1988). In the essays there are discussions that point back to his and other novels, and we can find fictional prototypes that we may modify for our own future anthropological and sociological genres.

In his reading of Broch's *Sleepwalkers*, Kundera (1988) shows the directions in which the novel—and we can generalize to the social sciences—is moving:

> The unachieved in [Broch's] work can show us the need for (1) a new art of *radical divestment* (which can encompass the complexity of existence in the modern world without losing architectonic clarity); (2) a new art of *novelistic counterpoint* (which can blend philosophy, narrative, and dream into one music); (3) a new art of the *specifically novelistic essay* (which does not claim to bear an apodictic message but remains hypothetical, playful, or ironic). (p. 65)

Bakhtin has argued that genres are complex representations of and forms for the way we experience the world. As compelling as this realist epistemology is to social scientists, Derrida (1981) subverts the whole notion of genre by showing that neither in their interior or at their boundaries are these insubstantial creatures firmly themselves; they elude classification at the very moment the critic begins to order them. Nevertheless through our received genres — the analytical book, the scholarly article, the essay, the evocative narrative ethnography — we attempt to gain a critical grasp on the most problematic phenomena of our time: our lives in the rapidly growing embrace of the cultures of capitalism.

Our texts will become a more sophisticated, multiple, heterophonic site of a struggle, just as are our lives in society.

One of the implications of the multigenre ethnography will be a transformation in reading, in graduate education, and in the subsequent conduct of inquiry:

(1) What we will read in graduate student socialization will include

    (a) the scholarly classics of the field and the current issues identified and debated in the scholarly books and journals;

    (b) relevant fictional literature, popular culture, television, movies, popular music, etc.; and

    (c) critical theory, whether in gender studies, film criticism, literary theory, philosophy, or adjacent cultural sciences.

(2) Out of this multigenre mix a new sort of enculturated student will be formed who will conceptualize fieldwork differently than now. *Above all, their inquiry might well have to acquire a narrative sort of quality, that is, students will seek to place themselves in unfolding situations, to live through complex ongoing events — the stuff of stories —* rather than looking alone for the meanings of gestures, the presentations of selves, class relations, the meaning of rituals, or other abstract, analytical category phenomena on which we historically have relied. Jackson (1989), elaborating on his radical empiricism helps make this point:

> Many of my most valued insights into Kuranko social life have followed from comparable cultivation and imitation of practical skills: hoeing on a farm, dancing (as one body), lighting a kerosene lantern properly, weaving a mat, consulting a diviner. To break the habit of using a linear communicational model for understanding bodily praxis, it is necessary to adopt a methodological strategy of joining in without ulterior motive and literally putting oneself in the place of other persons: inhabiting their world. Participation thus becomes an end in itself rather than a means of gathering closely observed data which will be subject to interpretation elsewhere *after the event.* (p. 135)

(3) From complex, across-the-human-sciences sort of reading, from leading lives of narrative inquiry, new multigenre textual constructions will appear. These will be montages of events and analyses connected by ideas, or events with digressive analytical and critical essays dominated by an authorial voice — either of the writer or of the subjects studied by the writer.

There are — to some, disturbing, to others, exhilarating — implications in a heterophonic ethnography: Multiple-genre writing (Ulmer, 1989) is a part of a massive reconfiguration of the human sciences and the once-secured disciplinary order of the university. We can already witness:

(1) the dissolution of boundaries between literature, sociology, anthropology, critical theory, philosophy, cinematography, computer science, and so on; and

(2) an ultimate transparency and probable liquidation of that series of sacred centers — those bodies of received and once firmly purchased ideas — that now constitute, somewhat precariously, each of the academic disciplines in the human sciences.

NOTES

1. Obviously in the telling I have simplified the history of the East India Company unconscionably. John Bruce (1810), not mentioning Linschoten, gave a number of reasons why the "John Company," as it came to be known in London, emerged when it did: The overland route beyond the Mediterranean had become too dangerous; Drake had returned in 1580 from a circumnavigation of the earth by way of the Cape of Good Hope showing the parvenu English that such a course could be navigated by Englishmen; Cavendish had duplicated Drake's feat six years later; and the merchants who wanted to incorporate as the London Company of Merchants had provided the Privy Council with a Memorial (read "intelligence report") on where the Portuguese settlements were and where the English might trade. Three ships were sent out with terrible losses, but one returned with impressive cargo captured from a Portuguese ship. "Whether it was from the information collected from these detached voyages to the East Indies, from the example of the associations . . . as having received the protection of the Crown, or from the Dutch . . . it is impossible to decide" (Bruce, 1810, p. 110).

2. Merchants comprised more than 85% of the representation of the East India Company at its inception. The gentry who were active in trade indulged on the whole more in colonization and exploration schemes (Robb, 1967).

3. "The Council, therefore, did act in a corporate fashion, and there is justification for saying that its promulgations influenced the history of Elizabethan England" (Ponko, 1968, p. 7).

4. Note that the entire program was framed by the perspective of the Papuan New Guineans after the introduction by the narrator. The voice of Nahua Rooney began with a critique, and the song by Ongka ended the show. Anthropologists and anthropology were set within the brackets of another cultural point of view. The Papuan voices were elicited, in a sense animated, and edited by our own public broadcasting network — station WGBH in Boston in particular. Is this us framing ourselves through the other? Yes, and it is in response to what we as ethnographers face in everyday life as we study peoples of various cultures. The editing and the airing were not farfetched constructions to viewers, but conveyed (as they were meant to) the air of reality: ourselves in the West verbally framed by peoples remote from us.

REFERENCES

Anonymous. (1807). *Free trade to the East Indies.* London: Chapple.

Bakhtin, M. M. (1981). *The dialogic imagination* (M. Holquist, Ed., C. Emerson & M. Holquist, Trans.). Austin: University of Texas Press.

Berreman, G. D. (1972). *Hindus of the Himalayas.* Berkeley: University of California Press.

Birdwood, G. & Foster, W. (Eds.). (1893). *The register of letters & c. of the governour and company of merchants of London trading into the East Indies 1600-1619.* London: Bernard Quaritch.

Boissevain, J. (1970). Fieldwork in Malta. In G. S. Spindler (Ed.), *Being an anthropologist* (pp. 58-84). New York: Holt, Rinehart and Winston.

Braudel, F. (1986). *The wheels of commerce.* New York: Harper and Row.

British Association for the Advancement of Science. (1841). *Report of the 1841 Meeting of the British Association for the Advancement of Science.* London: John Murray.

Broch, H. (1964). The sleepwalkers (W. Muir & E. Muir, Trans.). New York: Grosset and Dunlap. (Original work published 1932).

Bruce, J. (1810). *Annals of the honourable East India Company from their establishment by the charter of Queen Elizabeth, 1600, to the union of the London and English East India Companies 1707-8.* London: Cox, Son, and Baylis.

Buisine, A. (1981). The first eye. *Yale French Studies, 61,* 261-275.

Bulmer, M. (Ed.). (1982). *Social research ethics.* London: Macmillan.

Chandler, A. D., Jr. (1977). *The visible hand: The managerial revolution in American business.* Cambridge, MA: Harvard University Press.

Chernoff, J. M. (1979). *African rhythms and African sensibility.* Chicago: University of Chicago Press.

Clifford, J. (1983). On ethnographic authority. Representations, 2, 132-143.

Clifford, J. (1985). Histories of the tribal and modern. *Art in America, 73,* 164-76, 215.

Clifford, J., & Marcus, G. E. (Eds.). (1986). *Writing culture: The poetics and politics of ethnography.* Berkeley: University of California Press.

Conklin, H. (1964). A day in Parina. In J. B. Casagrande (Ed.), In the company of man (pp. 119-225). New York: Harper.

Cook, M. (1979). On the rim of the curve. In A. Fowler & A. Pittman (Eds.), *31 Newfoundland poets* (pp. 3-9). Newfoundland: Breakwater.

Derrida, J. (1981). The law of genre. In W. J. T. Mitchell (Ed.), On narrative (pp. 51-77). Chicago: University of Chicago Press.

Diamond, S. (1980). Anthropological traditions: The participants observed. In S. Diamond (Ed.), *Anthropology: Ancestors and heirs* (pp. 1-16). The Hague: Mouton.

Diamond, S. (1982). *Totems.* New York: Open Book/Station Hill.

Diamond, S. (1985). Return to the river. In I. Prattis (Ed.), *Reflections: The anthropological muse* (pp. 17-30). Washington, DC: American Anthropological Association.

Dorst, J. D. (1989). *The written suburb: An American site, an ethnographic dilemma.* Philadelphia: University of Pennsylvania Press.

Dumont, J. (1986). *Prologue to ethnography or prolegomena to anthropography. Ethos, 14,* 352-363.

62

Ellison, R. (1984). Interview by James Thompson, Lennox Raphael, and Steve Cannon, 1967. In *An American retrospective: Writings from Harper's Magazine 1850-1984.* New York: Harper's.

Evans-Pritchard, E. E. (1940). The Nuer. Oxford: Oxford University Press.

Evans-Pritchard, E. E. (1969). Preface. In J. Degerando, *The observation of savage peoples* (F. C. T. Moore, Trans.) Berkeley: University of California Press.

Feld, S. (1982). *Sound and sentiment.* Philadelphia: University of Pennsylvania Press.

Foster, G., Scudder, T., Colson, E., & Kemper, R. V. (Eds.). (1979). *Long-term field research in social anthropology.* New York: Academic Press.

Foucault, M. (1972). *The archaeology of knowledge and the discourse on language.* New York: Harper.

Gardner, B. (1971). *The East India Company.* New York: McCall.

Gargan, E. A. (1986). Zaire now dancing to different beat. *New York Times,* April 28.

Geertz, C. (1988). *Works and lives: The anthropologist as author.* Stanford, CA: Stanford University Press.

Glassie, H. (1982). *Passing the time in Ballymenone: Culture and history of an Ulster community.* Philadelphia: University of Pennsylvania Press.

Griffiths, P. (1974). *A license to trade: The history of English chartered companies.* London: Ernest Benn.

Hannerz, U. (1987, August). *Cosmopolitans and locals in world culture.* Paper presented to the First International Conference on the Olympics and East/West and South/North Cultural Exchanges in the World System, Seoul.

Jackson, M. (1986). *Barawa, and the way birds fly in the sky.* Washington, DC: Smithsonian Institution Press.

Jackson, M. (1989). *Paths toward a clearing: Radical empiricism and ethnographic inquiry.* Bloomington: University of Indiana Press.

Jay, M. (1984). *Adorno.* Cambridge, MA: Harvard University Press.

Kundera, M. (1988). *The art of the novel.* (L. Asher, Trans.). New York: Harper and Row.

Levy, R. I. (1973). *Tahitians: Mind and experience in the society islands.* Chicago: University of Chicago Press.

Linschoten, J. H. van (1970). The voyage of John Huygen van Linschoten to the East Indies. In *The Hakluyt Society First Series 70 and 71* (2 vols.). New York: Burt Franklin.

Lizot, J. (1985). *Tales of the Yanomami: Daily life in the Venezuelan forest.* Cambridge: Cambridge University Press.

Lutz, C. (1988). *Unnatural emotions: Everyday sentiments on a Micronesian atoll and their challenge to Western theory.* Chicago: University of Chicago Press.

Lynge, A. (1985). When my picture disappears. In I. Prattis (ed.), *Reflections: The anthropological muse* (p. 248). Washington, DC: American Anthropological Association.

MacCannell, D., & MacCannell, J. F. (1982). *The time of the sign.* Bloomington: Indiana University Press.

Maitland, F. (1958). Introduction. In O. Gierke, *Political theories of the Middle Age.* Boston: Beacon.

Malinowski, B. (1961). *Argonauts of the western Pacific.* New York: Dutton.

Malinowski, B. (1967). *A diary in the strict sense of the term.* London: Routledge and Kegan Paul.

Marcus, G. E., & Cushman, D. (1982). *Ethnographies as texts. Annual Review of Anthropology, 11,* 25-69.

Marcus, G. E., & Fischer, M. M. J. (1986). *Anthropology as cultural critique: An experimental moment in the human sciences.* Chicago: University of Chicago Press.

Morales, R. (1985). I am the reasonable one. In I. Prattis (Ed.), *Reflections: The anthropological muse.* (pp. 201-202). Washington, DC: American Anthropological Association.

Mukasa, H. (1975). *Sir Apolo Kagwa discovers Britain* (T. Liyong, Ed.). London: Heinemann.

Narayan, K. (1989). *Storytellers, saints, and scoundrels.* Philadelphia: University of Pennsylvania Press.

Ndebele, N. S. (1987). The English language and social change in South Africa. *Tri-Quarterly, 69,* 217-235.

NOVA. (1983, November). Anthropology on trial [Television episode]. Public Broadcasting System. Boston: Station WGBH.

Palmer, R. (1979). Liner notes. In P. Glass & R. Wilson, *Einstein on the Beach.* New York: CBS Records (MXT 38875).

Parks, M. (1986). Student king. *Philadelphia Inquirer,* April 27.

Ponko, V. Jr. (1968). The Privy Council and the spirit of Elizabethan economic management, 1558-1603. *Transactions of the American Philosophical Society* (N. S. Vol. 58, Part 4).

Powdermaker, H. (1966). *Stranger and friend: The way of an anthropologist.* New York: W. W. Norton.

Prattis, I. (Ed.). (1985). *Reflections: The anthropological muse.* Washington, DC: American Anthropological Association.

Price, R. (1983). *First-time: The historical vision of an Afro-American people.* Baltimore: Johns Hopkins University Press.

Reichel-Dolmatoff, G. (1971). *Amazonian cosmos: The sexual and religious symbolism of the Tukano Indians.* Chicago: University of Chicago Press.

Ridington, R. (1988). *Trail to heaven.* Iowa City: University of Iowa Press.

Robb, T. K. (1967). *Enterprise and empire: Merchant and gentry investment in the expansion of England, 1575-1630.* Cambridge, MA: Harvard University Press.

Rose, D. (1986). Transformations of disciplines through their texts. *Cultural Anthropology, 1,* 317-327.

Rose, D. (1987). *Black American street life: South Philadelphia, 1969-1971.* Philadelphia: University of Pennsylvania Press.

Rose, D. (1989). *Patterns of American culture: Ethnography and estrangement.* Philadelphia: University of Pennsylvania Press.

Royal Anthropological Institute. (1951). *Notes and queries on anthropology* (6th ed.). London: Routledge and Kegan Paul.

Said, E. W. (1989). Representing the colonized: Anthropology's interlocutors. *Critical Inquiry, 15,* 205-225.

Seeger, A. (1981). *Nature and society in Brazil.* Cambridge: Harvard University Press.

Shostak, M. (1983). *Nisa, the life and words of a !Kung woman.* New York: Vintage Press.

Stack, C. B. (1974). *All our kin.* New York: Harper and Row.

Stoller, P. (1984). Eye, mind and word in anthropology. *L'Homme, 24,* 93-114.

Stoller, P. (1989a). *The fusion of the worlds.* Chicago: University of Chicago Press.

Stoller, P. (1989b). *The taste of ethnographic things: The senses in anthropology.* Philadelphia: University of Pennsylvania Press.

Stoller, P., & Olkes, C. (1987). *In sorcery's shadow.* Chicago: University of Chicago Press.

64

Strachan, M., & Penrose, B. (1971). *The East India Company journals of Captain William Keeling and Master Thomas Bonner, 1615-1617.* Minneapolis: University of Minnesota Press.

Szwed, J. F. (1980). Josef Skvorecky and jazz literature. *World Literature Today, 54,* 586-590.

Taubman, P. (1986). *Through a soviet lense: Gomorrah on Hudson. New York Times,* April 2.

Tedlock, D. (1983). *The spoken word and the work of interpretation.* Philadelphia: University of Pennsylvania Press.

Uberoi, J. P. S. (1978). *Science and culture.* Delhi: Oxford University Press.

Ulmer, G. (1989). *Teletheory: Grammatology in the age of video.* New York: Routledge and Kegan Paul.

Wagner, R. (1975). *The invention of culture.* Englewood Cliffs, NJ: Prentice-Hall.

Whyte, W. F. (1955). Street corner society (2nd ed.). Chicago: University of Chicago Press.

ABOUT THE AUTHOR

DAN ROSE teaches ethnography at the University of Pennsylvania, where he is a professor of landscape architecture and of anthropology. He is the author of *Black American Street Life* and *Patterns of American Culture,* numerous articles, and several books of poetry. He is a founding editor of the Series in Contemporary Ethnography at the University of Pennsylvania Press and serves on a number of journal editorial boards. Fieldwork has been conducted among African-Americans, ethnic middle-class business-men, and upper-class residents of an estate area who pursue the various sports associated with horsemanship. Most recently his field research has been among members of the boardrooms of the country's largest corpora-tions, especially in the manufacturing and financial services sectors. His inquiries into American life at these several levels have focused consistently on the culture of the marketplace.